SACRED
LEAVES

A Magical Guide to
Orisha Herbal Witchcraft

About the Author

Diego de Oxóssi is a gaucho based in São Paulo Brazil. He is a priest of Kimbanda and Babalosha of Candomblé, working with personal development, consulting, and spiritual guidance throughout Brazil and abroad. For more than 20 years, Diego de Oshossi has been dedicated to researching and presenting courses, lectures, and workshops on Afro-Brazilian religions, their regional forms of expression, and the integration of their rituals into society.

In 2015 he released his first book, *Desvendando Exu* (published in English as *Traditional Brazilian Black Magic* by Destiny Books, 2021). This work demystifies the controversial character of African-origin religions and shows that Eshu is a friend, defender, and companion of his faithful. *Sacred Leaves* is based on three books originally published in Portuguese in 2016 and 2018.

Diego's latest book, *Odus de Nascimento (Birth Odus: Unveil Your Personality with the Astrological Chart of the Orishas)* was published in 2020. This work teaches the secrets and mysteries of African astrology while taking the reader on an inner journey of soul growing and awareness.

SACRED LEAVES

A Magical Guide to
ORISHA HERBAL WITCHCRAFT

DIEGO DE OXÓSSI

Llewellyn Publications
Woodbury, Minnesota

First Edition
First Printing, 2022

Book design by Colleen McLaren
Cover design by Kevin R. Brown
Translated by Marisa Schaurich

Llewellyn Publications is a registered trademark of Llewellyn Worldwide Ltd.

Library of Congress Cataloging-in-Publication Data
Names: Oxóssi, Diego de, author. | Oxóssi, Diego de, Folhas
    sagradas.
Title: Sacred leaves : a magical guide to orisha herbal witchcraft / Diego
    de Oxóssi.
Description: First edition. | Woodbuy, Minnesota : Llewellyn Worldwide,
    Ltd, 2022. | "Between 2016 and 2018, Diego de Oxóssi wrote and
    published the trilogy As Folhas Sagradas: Poderes, Magias e Segredos-
    which had its copyrights sold abroad for publication in English, as
    Sacred Leaves, by Llewellyn Worldwide" — About the author.
Identifiers: LCCN 2022011651 (print) | LCCN 2022011652 (ebook) | ISBN
    9780738767055 (paperback) | ISBN 9780738767215 (ebook)
Subjects: LCSH: Herbs—Therapeutic use—Brazil. | Herbs—Brazil—Religious
    aspects. | Botany, Medical—Brazil. | Afro-Brazilian cults. | Black
    people—Brazil—Religion. | Medicine, Magic, mystic, and
    spagiric—Brazil. | Materia medica, Vegetable. | Candomblé
    (Religion)—Brazil. | Umbanda (Cult)—Brazil. |
    Brazil—Civilization—African influences.
Classification: LCC RM666.H33 O985 2022 (print) | LCC RM666.H33 (ebook) |
    DDC 615.3/21—dc23/eng/20220414
LC record available at https://lccn.loc.gov/2022011651
LC ebook record available at https://lccn.loc.gov/2022011652

Llewellyn Publications
A Division of Llewellyn Worldwide Ltd.
2143 Wooddale Drive
Woodbury, MN 55125-2989
www.llewellyn.com

Printed in the United States of America

Other Books by Diego de Oxóssi

Traditional Brazilian Black Magic (Destiny Books, 2021)

Afro-Brazilian Numerology: Awakening Your Better Self with the Wisdom of the Orishas (Destiny Books, 2022)

Forthcoming Books by Diego de Oxóssi

African Destiny (Rockpool Australia, 2023)

Ewé njé
Ògún njé
Ògún to ò je
Ewé re ni kò pe

Leaves work
Remedies work
If a remedy does not work
it's because a leaf is missing

Contents

Contents

Dedication

Publishing a special edition of the *Sacred Leaves* trilogy in a single volume, seeing its titles reach the mark of almost ten thousand copies sold, and having them translated worldwide: it's a dream come true and affirmation that life is good and worthwhile. For this reason, this work is dedicated to my mother, Marines, and my sister, Camila, who, even from a distance, always found ways to allow me to dream and to make these dreams come true.

To Mãe Ieda de Ogun, for all the affection and companionship in these years of the journey together, for the simplicity in her words, for trust, and, especially, for conversations before bedtime in August 2016.

And also to the warrior Anderson de Ogun, a fellow on this journey, who, with a sword in hand, gave me strength and courage to resist all challenges.

To my dear friend Claudiney Prieto, who kindly prefaced the first Portuguese edition of *O Poder das Folhas* (*The Power of Leaves*)—the book that began the trilogy and the special edition you now have in your hands—and who, with his pioneering spirit and the courage to bring witchcraft into his life, was the inspiration for my first steps in magic.

To Eshu Tiriri Lonã, for guiding my paths since forever and until now. And to *bàbá mi* Odé Funmilaiyo, for inspiring me every single day and indicating the direction in which I, his single arrow, should go. To Eshu 7 Facadas—my best friend, my drinking buddy, and my eternal guardian—for all: for the Kingdom, for the world, for existing in my paths!

And in the name of Eshu, to all those who encouraged me and all who doubted—both are my daily fuel.

Gratitude and Abundance!

Preface

S ince ancient times and in all the magical traditions of the world, nature has been a source of healing for the body and soul, and what I'm going to tell you now will change the way you see even the simplest plant species that grow in your garden or appear in pots and floral arrangements. Earth, air, fire, and water: each leaf, flower, root, and seed carries energies within itself that represent the Universe, reflecting the mysteries of life in its saps and scents.

In African and Afro-Amerindian traditions, it is no different! *"Kosi ewe, kosi orisa"*—without a leaf, there is no Orisha. This was the first and most important lesson I learned in nearly fifteen years of priesthood. The "green blood" of the leaves is used from the first spiritual cleansing and herbal bath to the most complex rituals worshipping the African gods, in which their divine particles are literally rooted inside the bodies of neophytes in a process of magical rebirth.

Male and female leaves, active potential and passive potential that complement each other and that sometimes move apart and nullify one another. The smell of smoke and burning incense that is capable of enchanting or intoxicating. Healing and cursing spell powders. Baths with the right leaves, capable of bringing to the world the manifestation of the gods and goddesses through mediumistic incorporation...

Speaking like this, it may seem that the use of sacred leaves is something restricted to those who have gone through very difficult and secret initiation processes. The truth, however, is that herbal powers, magic, and secrets can be awakened by anyone with faith and gratitude for the charms that nature offers us and can be used in your daily rituals, helping you to discover your personal purpose and transform the reality around you.

Perhaps you've read or heard all of this before. Perhaps you've even taken the first steps in some tradition of natural magic. What most people don't know—and those who know usually don't tell—is that each herb has within it several different powers. Precisely for that reason, there are techniques and fundamentals one should learn to awaken the desired potential of a plant, determining your magical success in every ritual.

When I first realized that everything around us is made of pure energy and that it is possible to access this energy to vibrate together with it in pursuit of my biggest and best goals, I discovered the biggest secret of all: the gods and goddesses live within us and within every living being, animal or plant. More than that: each one of us is a sleeping deity waiting to wake up.

That was the real turning point in my life, and as you experience the teachings in this book, I sincerely hope it becomes yours too!

In *Sacred Leaves* we will learn how to identify and classify plants and leaves using their magical characteristics: shape, smell, color, vibration, and the ruling Orisha of each one. By understanding how and for what each of them works, we will learn to combine their powers with the elements of nature, the days of the week, the vibration of the planets, and the phases of the moon to enhance the results of your rituals. Along with this, we will learn in detail how to do the sacred harvest of the ingredients for magical rituals, entering the realm of Ossain, the Orisha's healer, and then, returning to the city, we will learn how to create a magical garden at home and how to sing to enchant and awaken the inner secrets of the leaves by using words of power.

Like a leafy tree that slowly germinates and grows to great heights, each of these lessons will be a new step on your journey to explore the herbal witchcraft of the Orishas. All of this, however, is often done without knowing it—after all, the magic is in everything and everyone around us! Therefore, in the second half of the first part of the book, we will cross the oceans between African and Asian traditions to unveil the mysteries of magic in day-to-day life.

From there, you will discover how the wisdom of feng shui and Roma magic can be combined with African witchcraft to create pots of power with the most diverse goals, such as love and success. In addition, the mysteries of aromatherapy and magical cookery will also be part of our journey, and we will discover that even small things that seem to have no importance— such as growing a pot at the entrance of our home or on our porch, flavoring food when cooking, and choosing the right perfume for a date or work meeting, for example—can become true and powerful rituals.

At the end of our journey, we will have traveled around the world and experienced a little of the magical traditions of Africa, Asia, Europe, and the Americas. Therefore, the second half of the book brings you a collection of 365 plant species, classified in detail by their powers and their characteristics for magical combination through their ruling Orishas, like a true dictionary of herbal witchcraft. With this, you will have at your disposal the tools you need to substitute some exotic ingredients with others that can be easily found anywhere in the world.

To conclude, at the end of the book you will find an herbal grimoire with recipes for magical bathing; instructions for fumigations, or making aromatic and purifying smoke; directions for making the traditional powders and soaps of the Orishas, power pots, and Roma perfumes; and complete rituals to perform at home or at work that will put into practice everything learned on this journey with herbal magic!

For all this, it is with honor and joy that I now place the key of magic into your hands! Let's unravel the mysteries together.

Foreword

In a time without medicine, when the technology we currently know didn't exist, the use of herbs and plants was the only possible way of curing the body and soul. It is difficult to pinpoint the moment when men discovered that plants had medicinal properties. Trial and error likely led to this discovery, and the observation of animals' behavior around certain herbs is also one of the possible ways in which humans began identifying and using some of them for their healing properties.

No matter the origin of the art of healing through plants, one thing is certain: they have always been considered sacred and divine! Herbs carried the power of the gods, and through proper use and manipulation by those who knew how to awaken their powers, they became true elixirs that could close wounds, lower fevers, and relieve pain. They could raise up or bring down everybody from the most humble commoner to the most powerful king and queen. They were thus not only instruments of healing, but also of magic.

The ancient science of plant use has survived time and has been passed on to us by the wise guardians of this hidden wisdom, from generation to generation. Who has not put a piece of rue behind their ear to ward off the evil eye and illness? And who among us has not asked family members for our grandmother's miracle recipe, kept under lock and key, that cures a bad case of the flu?

Many of the ancient herbal potions are still in use today. Melissa water to help calm, rose milk to cleanse the skin, and chamomile tea to lighten the hair are just a small sample of the benefits of this wisdom that has developed over the centuries, wisdom that was undoubtedly considered magical when we didn't have the scientific knowledge we have today.

Even in the midst of tremendous advances in science, the interest in the magical and medicinal use of plants has grown every day. This same science, which constantly seeks to discredit the metaphysical powers of magic, has ironically contributed to proving that certain compounds extracted from plants act on an energetic, mental, and emotional level to harmonize and aid people's well-being. After all, what is magic if not the ability to manipulate principles and substances in order to bring about changes at different levels?

This occult herbal knowledge has always been at the center of magical and ecstatic religions, making plants cursed, blessed, sacred, or forbidden according to their specific properties. However, only the initiated few knew their true meaning, which has been the subject of numerous legends and myths.

My own religious tradition, Wicca, attributes the sharing of this knowledge with humans to divine intervention. Legends tell that the Celtic king Nuada, who ruled the Tuatha Dé Danann (the "tribe of the gods"), lost one of his arms. According to their precepts, any king who acquired any kind of deformity was obliged to renounce the throne. The goddess Airmid's father, Dian Cecht, was the gods' chief physician and created an arm made of silver for the king that allowed him to rule again.

However, Miach, the son of Dian Cecht, knew that it was possible, with his surgical skill and the magical ability of his sister Airmid, to use an even better solution to regenerate Nuada's arm completely. Together, sister and brother perfectly reconstituted the flesh of Nuada's arm, "three times, for three days and three nights," with the use of sacred herbs accompanied by magical words, powerful incantations, and magic. When Dian Cecht realized that his son had surpassed his own skills, he became enraged and killed Miach with a blow to the head.

Deeply saddened, Airmid went to her brother's tomb and circled the grave with stones. The young goddess, overcome with grief, wept bitter tears at the burial of her brother Miach. Drops of her tears fell on the ground, and shortly thereafter, Airmid noticed that new life started to sprout from the earth. Three hundred and sixty-five herbs began to grow in that place, each of them revealing itself as a cure for a specific part of the body.

Airmid, realizing that her brother had sent a legacy to share with everyone, laid her cloak on the ground to begin to organize and classify the herbs according to their use. She paid particular attention to where each of the herbs came from and where it was collected, and she cataloged each according to its properties. When Dian Cecht became aware of this, once again in a fury of rage, he picked up the cloak and scattered all the leaves to the wind, losing forever the gift that Miach would share with humanity through his beloved sister. Only Airmid knows the mysteries each leaf holds.

Legends say that to this day Airmid wanders the world, teaching the medicinal secrets of herbs to those who will listen to them and seek her knowledge in forest clearings and the deep woods. Therefore, when necessary, we invoke her spirit as a guide in this task. The number of herbs that the goddess cataloged—365—is a symbol of the death of a year, which reminds us that when we do not find herbs that are able to heal us, only time can close our wounds.

Legends like this abound in many cultures. They show us that the art of healing and enchanting through the use of plants is available to all of us. The gods are all the time whispering in our ears the wisdom of every leaf. Go to a forest or a park, sit at the foot of a tree, and listen to the sound of the wind blowing through the leaves, and you will surely come to the conclusion that trees can talk. By listening to them, you reclaim the ancient wisdom of magic and healing that belongs to all humanity.

The book now in your hands is one of the depositories of that legacy. In *Sacred Leaves*, Diego de Oxóssi shares information about the use of herbs from the perspectives of different spiritual cultures and traditions. No matter what your religion or your perception of the Divine, here you will find invaluable references that can be used by you to access the magical power of herbs and take advantage of their vibration and energy. This book carries an ancestral wisdom, which can be used with all the support that only a source of references like this can provide.

This book is like a tree full of leaves that reveal to you the ancestral memory of the world's soul, linking heaven and earth. Each line brings a revelation, each leaf a piece of knowledge. Enter now into the sacred wood and let the gods sing in the forest of your soul while you read the wisdom written on each of these pages. Come closer, take a seat, and your mind will become like a rooted tree from which new buds will bloom from old branches.

Claudiney Prieto
Best-selling author of *Wicca: A Religião das Deusa*
(*Wicca: The Religion of the Goddess*)

Introduction: A Bit of History

S ince the arrival of the first enslaved Black people in Brazil, in the mid-1500s, traditional medicine and natural medicine have been mixed in the heart of communities. Even before that, the magical and therapeutic properties of plants were already known through contact with the indigenous people who lived here and had found in nature their means of existence and subsistence.

However, it was through the first organizations of Candomblé—the name given to the religion based on African gods practiced in northeast Brazil—that these practices gained special notoriety for their magical character. In the migration from the countryside to the city, the formation of the *terreiros*—the temples where Candomblé is practiced—was characterized not only by the establishment of places to worship the Orishas, but also by the creation of a "place of memory, origins, and traditions, where, in addition to preserving a ritualistic knowledge and an ancestral language ... life is celebrated in a very particular way,"[1] according to José Flávio Pessoa de Barros. Regarding the process of slavery and the cultural resignification of enslaved Africans, it is also important to notice that:

> Of the six million Africans who survived oceanic crossings to the Americas, four million landed in Brazil and were deliberately separated from their original ethnicities and consanguineous families to prevent their

---

1. José Flávio Pessoa de Barros, *A Floresta Sagrada de Ossain: O Segredo das Folhas* (Rio de Janeiro: Pallas, 2011). Translated from the Portuguese.

1

social reorganization and possible revolt. This did not, however, prevent Blacks from forming a new group, reidentifying themselves by their shared enslavement, skin color, and spiritual practices. Though their religious practices differed among themselves, these practices contained within them common elements of worship to divinized ancestors and the forces of nature. In addition, the reception of these reorganized groups under the aegis of the confraternities and brotherhoods of the Catholic Church at the time contributed to this unification, maintenance, and redefinition of spirituality, now under the syncretized mantle of the Catholic saints. ...

The process of black organization and reidentification through religion occurred throughout America. It is right to say that the Voodoo of Haiti, the Santeria of Cuba and the Caribbean, the Regla de Palo of the Dominican Republic and Puerto Rico, the cult of Maria Lionza in Venezuela, and the calundus of Brazil, which later would evolve into the Bahian Candomblé, are essentially the same practice, each adapted to the particular geography, culture, and available resources of each country and region into which they were inserted. ...

This distribution of slave labor and the consequent social reconfigurations gave rise to the various expressions of African-origin religions in the country [Brazil, due to its geographic size]: Candomblé in Bahia, Nagô or Xangô in Pernambuco, Tambor de Mina in Maranhão, Macumba in Rio de Janeiro, and Batuque in Rio Grande do Sul, among others.[2]

---

2. Diego de Oxóssi, *Traditional Brazilian Black Magic: The Secrets of Kimbanda Magicians* (Rochester, VT: Destiny Books, 2021).

As a result, enslaved African people—due to the need to adapt to the New World—reformulated a series of customs and rites, added to their original culture several aspects of what they found in their new land through contact with natives and Europeans, and discovered new ingredients and ways to work with these natural elements that, despite a climate similar to Africa, differed in various aspects of production and supply.

One of the most important works regarding the classification of African plant species was written at the end of the nineteenth century by the Count of Ficalho. According to Barros, the Count considers that, as far as East Africa is concerned, the dissemination of plant species—mainly of Asian origin—was caused by the Arabs during the tenth century. In West Africa, on the other hand, this task fell to the Portuguese, who had exercised economic and political domination there since the sixteenth century.[3] The separation of these Eastern and Western influences, rather than being the result of war, was due to geographical issues and difficulties in territorial advancement because of natural barriers such as deserts and mountains.

Even so, before the European presence on the African continent, there were already networks of trade and trafficking in food, plants, spices, and other consumer goods:

> There was thus a network of trade routes that connected cities and villages across almost all of West Africa, between the Sahara and the coast. Regular markets were held. ... The operations of the Mandinka, Hausa, and Yoruba merchants were truly international.[4]

---

3. Barros, *A Floresta Sagrada de Ossain*.
4. Roland Oliver and J. D. Fage, *Breve História de África* (Lisboa: Sa da Costa, 1980), in Barros, *A Floresta Sagrada de Ossain*.

Once more according to Barros, it was the discovery of the New World, however, that had the greatest influence on the introduction of previously unknown plant species to the African continent:

> America was a rich source of new useful plants … The varied vegetation of the American tropics, and their natural products, were studied with interest and sometimes with true scientific spirit by Spanish travelers and writers … The seeds of interesting species came to Europe, and some flourished in the climate of Spain and Portugal, as happened with corn and peppers. Others, however, required greater heat; their cultivation in temperate climates was impossible, but they could develop in the tropics of Africa and Asia, where they were taken.[5]

Also, as I explain in my first book released in English, titled *Traditional Brazilian Black Magic*:

> The history of the discovery and colonization of Brazil [and all Americas] is intertwined with the history of the African diaspora and the slave system that was practiced all over the world. While Europe since ancient times has been the cultural center of the West, Africa has been the commercial center. … Even when the trade market shifted to Asia in the Middle Ages, the African continent remained an important commerce source. By the middle of the thirteenth century, Italy had expanded its commercial activities and dominated trade in the

---

5. Conde de Ficalho, *Plantas Úteis da África Portuguesa* (Lisboa: Divisão de Publicaðcões e Biblioteca, Agência General das Colónias, 1947), in Barros, *A Floresta Sagrada de Ossain*.

Mediterranean and beyond. Inspired by Italy's activities and success, and with the aim of dominating trade or at least eliminating intermediaries, the Portuguese became pioneers in navigation and exploration, establishing a multicontinental trading system and becoming the world's main economic power.[6]

With that, it is possible to see that the plants currently known in the Americas and used in all ways—be they culinary, medicinal, or magical—have, in fact, come from all over the world. The slave trade, as well as the commercial and imperialist voyages from the fifteenth to the eighteenth centuries, were determining factors for this redefinition of Brazil's flora, which already had an abundance of native species. Like its culture and people, the country's flora absorbed new elements that had to adapt to the reality of their land for the continuation of life.

On the correlation between magic and cooking in African lands, especially on the introduction of agriculture in Yoruba society, Barros states that this was "considered primarily the responsibility of the women. Agricultural activity was, however, related to magical rituals, which gave women a prominent position in the social organization, since they were the depositaries of the secrets that favored the harvest."[7]

Specifically, regarding the use of plants in Candomblé rituals, it is also essential to emphasize the importance of the religious and cultural exchanges made by Iyá Nassô, an enslaved African woman responsible for founding the first Candomblé of Ketu nation in Brazil; Bámgbósé Obitikó, a free African man from the Ketu nation in the company of Obatossi, goddaughter of

---

6. Oxóssi, *Traditional Brazilian Black Magic*.

7. Barros, *A Floresta Sagrada de Ossain*.

5

Iyá Nassô; Balbino Daniel de Paula, also known as Obaraim, a renowned Orishas priest; and Pierre Fatumbi Verger, an illustrious French researcher who settled in Brazil and who contributed a lot to Afro-religious literature.

PART ONE

The Magical
Uses of Plants

CHAPTER 1

Ossain: The Doctor of Body & Soul in African Magic

African religious beliefs and practices, established for many years in Brazil under various forms of expression, are based on the spirits known as Orishas—forces of nature that concentrate and represent in themselves everything that makes up the Universe. Each Orisha has its field of action, its characteristic elements, its representative form, and its correct ways to be praised and given offerings—or, better said, gifts.

Ossain—known in Afro-Caribbean traditions as Agwe—is the Orisha responsible for all existing leaves, fruits, and vegetables. He is the great healer and sorcerer of the African pantheon, showing even then the intrinsic relationship between medicine and magic. Of all the Orishas, he is the one who knows the deepest secrets of plants and how to use them correctly for one purpose or another; after all, even the strongest of poisons can, in the right dosage, serve as a cure.

From a magical point of view, every malaise, physical or spiritual, is considered a disease, and it is therefore necessary to find healing through magical rituals called *ebós*. Thus, we must turn to Ossain whenever we wish to use plants and their parts in the composition of magical works, asking him for authorization for the ritual and calling on him to allow that element's magical power to be activated and achieve its objective.

A traditional African *itan*—the name given to the legends and myths of the Orishas—explains how even though every Orisha rules his or her own plants, all of the plants belong to Ossain:

Ossain used to keep his leaves in a gourd and didn't teach anyone his secrets. The Orishas, when they wanted a leaf, had to ask him. Oshossi, then, complained to Oya that whenever he needed a leaf he had to beg Ossain. Oya, feeling sorry for him, said she would do something and started to shake her skirts, making a gale. The wind knocked over Ossain's gourd, making the leaves scatter everywhere. Then, the Orishas ran to get the leaves, and each one of them took their own.[8]

It is important to highlight, however, that even though each Orisha picked up his or her leaves and took possession of them, none of them knew the correct way to enchant them and activate their power. Oya's winds scattered the leaves over the earth, but all of them remained dormant. How to awaken them is Ossain's great secret, as is the use of plants in magical rituals—and this secret, he doesn't give it away to anyone. Another *itan* of Ossain's tells us how Ossain and Orunmila, the god of wisdom, became close:

When Orunmila came into the world, he asked for a slave to plow his field; one was bought in the market: it was Ossain. When it was time to begin his work, Ossain realized that he was going to cut the herb that would cure the fever. And then he shouted: "It is impossible to cut this herb, as it is very useful." The second one cured headaches. He also refused to destroy it. The third treated colic. "Indeed," he said, "I can't pull out such necessary herbs." Orunmila, learning of his slave's conduct, expressed a desire to see these herbs, which he then refused to have cut and which were deemed of great value, as they

---

8. Barros, *A Floresta Sagrada de Ossain.*

contributed to keeping the body in good health. He then decided that Ossain should stay close to him to explain the virtues of plants, leaves, and herbs, keeping him always by his side at the time of consultations.[9]

For this reason, to this day it is necessary to praise Ossain before performing any Orisha herbal rituals and, through the correct incantations, to awaken the plants so that they have *ashé*—the magical force for them to fulfill the wishes and objectives of those who manipulate them. This story is also important because it emphasizes Ossain's playful and mischievous character, very similar to Orisha Eshu: even after having lost absolute dominion over the leaves to other Orishas, he still remained indispensable, because he was the only one who knew the magic that they carry within them.

---

9. Pierre Fatumbi Verger, *Orishas: Deuses Iorubas na África e no Novo Mundo*, 6th ed., trans. Cida Nóbrega (Salvador: Corrupio, 2002), 123. Translated from the Portuguese.

CHAPTER 2

Physical Characteristics of Plants

B efore we begin to understand the magical aspects of herbs, seeds, and plants, we need to understand their physical structure—because, in many cases, each part will fulfill different goals. In general, plants can be classified into six parts of their physical structure—just like the human body. So, all plants can be divided and identified as follows:

1. Seed
2. Root, underground stem, or rhizome
3. Stem or trunk—from which the bark and bulb can be separated, as well as the branches
4. Leaves
5. Fruits
6. Flowers

Botany is the field of biology dedicated to the plant kingdom. It studies the various aspects that make up plants, such as morphology, classification, identification, reproduction, physiology, distribution, and the relationship between plant species and other living beings.

From the perspective of botany, plants are classified according to the organization of the body, the tissues that transport sap, and the reproductive organs. In addition, all of botany's research objects—that is, all plants—are also subject to a classification logic called *taxonomic scheme*—a form of universal organization of all living things under a very rigid hierarchy, from which one then arrives at an individual organism's scientific name.

However, none of these classifications are able to determine the magical, medicinal, or therapeutic use of these species since they focus on *scientific* study and classification and look only at *what can be proven by traditional research methods.*

In the magical use of plants—whether for the composition of baths, fumigations, powders, or perfumes—each of these parts will have different values and pertinence and may or may not be used together in the same recipe. Besides this, the parameters for identifying, recognizing, and classifying the magical aspects of each species are more subtle, allowing the grouping and resignification of its elements according to the ritual's objectives. Nevertheless, it is important to emphasize that the scientific name and the parameters of classification and ordering of living things under the taxonomic scheme are of fundamental importance for species to be found and identified worldwide. Also, in the scientific names defined by the taxonomic scheme it is possible to find references that will serve as a guide for the grouping and substitution of some ingredients in our rituals and spells, as we'll learn in later chapters.

CHAPTER 3

Magical Classification of Species

In contrast with the botanical point of view, from a magical and therapeutic perspective, especially in African culture, plants are classified in a much more sensible way. It is from these new classification parameters that we will be able to define the healing properties of plants, whether for physical healing or spiritual healing. By the way, it is important to recognize a cultural issue linked to African spirituality that is very important in the use of plants for baths and fumigations:

> The ritual cleansing and purification ... are performed with an odd number of plant species (one, three, seven) and aim to cancel the disorder resulting from a state of "disease." This state, however, does not refer only to physiological disturbances, but, above all, to the disruption of the connection (lack of communication) necessary for the well-being (health) between the *ará ayé* ["physical body"] and the *ará orun* ["spiritual body"], between the fundamental complementary binary opposition, between life and death, between the natural and the supernatural.
>
> In short, disorder is equal to disease (physical and/or social malaise). The return to order is propitiated by the action that inequality (odd quantity of ingredients) produces; the change of state from "disease" to "health" implies, therefore, inequality in the same way that order/balance supposes equality (odd quantity of ingredients).[10]

---

10. Barros, *A Floresta Sagrada de Ossain*.

It is clear, then, that any type of physical or spiritual imbalance is considered a disease, which presupposes the need for healing through the rituals of bathing, fumigating, and magical rituals, or *ebós*. The energetic imbalance is caused by an excess or deficiency of a particular vibration and energy in our spiritual body, which ends up being reflected in the physical body. Thus, some recipes will be formed by activating energies, to supply the deficiencies, while others will be formed by deactivating energies, to balance the excesses.

In this way, the classification of plants according to African magic will be made through the following parameters:

- Size
- Color
- Shape
- Smell
- Taste
- Element of nature
- Vibration
- Energy

Based on these parameters, recipes for baths and fumigations will be created under the rules of energetic balance and imbalance that we will learn later on. It is also through them that it will be possible to substitute one plant with another, if for any reason you don't have access to a specific ingredient in a magical recipe.

Size

Regarding size, plant species can be classified into three main groups: *igi*, *kékéré*, and *àfòmó*. Of these three, the most varied and complex is the *kékéré*.

In the category of *igi* there are medium and large trees, home to various energies, including the Ancestors and some Orishas. Among them, seven main ones stand out, considered the "pillars of the world": *Igi Osé* (baobab), *Akóko* (Akoko tree or African border tree), *Ódàn* (wild fig tree), *Orógbó* (bitter kola), *Apáòká* (African mahogany), *Ekikà* (hog plum or yellow mombin), and *Ìrókò* (Iroko tree or African teak). Beyond these, other species also deserve to be mentioned: *Topónúrìn* (jackfruit), *Àtòri* (Atori tree, Glyphaea brevis), *Àgbaó* (silver cecropia), *Igi Àta* (prickly ash), *Adankó* (bamboo), *Ìpèsán* (American muskwood), and *Igi Òpè* (African oil palm, also called Màrìwò).

The category of *kékéré*, in turn, covers a diverse set of small-sized species, shrubs, ground plants, herbs, and sessile plants (whose leaves are attached directly to the plant's stem). It is in this category that all the other aspects of magical classification will focus: color, shape, smell, taste, element of nature, vibration, and energy.

The category of *àfòmó* comprises climbing or creeping plants and parasites, which depend symbiotically on other species to survive and thus exploit their hosts. Therefore, we can infer that, for the most part, the plants considered àfòmó are classified as red, of the fire or earth element, hot, and male.

Color

The classification of plants based on their color must first be understood symbolically. Much more than a plant's physical color—although this is obviously an objective distinguishing characteristic—this classification is made through the symbolism that the three primary colors of African rituals have: white, or *funfun*; red, or *pupa*; and black, or *dundun*.

White is, in the Orishas herbal witchcraft tradition, the color of purity, calm, and the principle of creation. For this reason, it is attributed above all to Oshala and the other Orishas responsible for the creation of the world and, consequently, is associated with the elements of water and air, especially the second. Thus, in addition to the visual colors that plants can present, the color classification also obeys these criteria, with all plants belonging to Oshala, Oshoguian, Yemaya, and Nana being considered white—or *funfun*.

In turn, the color red—*pupa* in the Yoruba language—has a series of positive and negative symbolisms. It is the color of the Orishas Eshu, Shango, and Oya, and it represents movement, activation, and the beginning of something; disorder and chaos; blood flow; and the dynamism necessary to achieve objectives. In addition, it is the color associated with the elements of fire and earth. Thus, it is possible to affirm that all Orishas, male and female, are responsible for plants classified as red, with the exception of Oshala.

Black, however, is a delicate classification and is rarely mentioned in the literature on African culture and magic, being generally associated with death, evil witchcraft, and all that is dark and harmful—including, in the context of plants, all those that are poisonous, thorny, and harmful in some way. Most of the time the plants classified as *dundun* are linked to the Orishas Eshu, Nana, Babaluaiye, Egun, and Iku (Death itself, which is also considered an Orisha).

Further, the shade of each species' main color is also considered in this classification and is associated with its energy—that is, the opposing and complementary male-female principle. Thus, dark-colored species are usually associated with male Orishas, called *Oborós*, while light-colored species are associated with female Orishas, called *Iyabás*. An exception to this rule are the plants belonging to Nana, the Ancient Mother of Creation, who has violet and dark purple under her domain, such as the plants *taioba* (arrowleaf elephant ear) and *viuvinha* (queen's wreath vine).

Shape

The principle of complementarity is what defines all the criteria for classifying plants. With this, it is necessary to remember that they all take into consideration an essential rule: the balance between male-female or positive-negative complementary pairs.

This division of complementary pairs can be easily done in the category of shape, as well as in the category of texture. The plants with an elongated shape, which are pointed or sharp, which are rough or rugged in texture, and which resemble knives and swords in shape, are related to the mythical figure of the phallus and, in turn, are considered hot and warlike—belonging to the male Orishas. Those with a round or sinuous shape, which are moist or with a soft texture, are considered cold and peaceful and are under the domain of the female Orishas or of Oshala. Barros reports, about his experience with the herbalists of Bahia, that "if, perhaps, the species [elongated, pointed, or hot] were also attributed to a female deity, immediately its bellicose aspect would be mentioned"[11]—such as Oya or Oshun Opara and Oshun Iponda, two faces of Oshun, the goddess of love and beauty.

Smell and Taste

Just like with the classification by its shape, a plant's smell and taste will characterize it within one or another group of complementary pairs. In this way, the aroma given off when its leaves are rubbed is evaluated: a soft or sweet aroma is classified as female, while an acrid and intense aroma is classified as

---

11. Barros, *A Floresta Sagrada de Ossain*, 50.

male. Likewise, spicy, bitter, and salty flavors will be male, while sweet, sour, bittersweet, and mild flavors are considered female.

Element of Nature

All Western magic traditions have their basis in nature and the primary alchemic elements: air, fire, water, and earth. As in the Yoruba tradition, European witchcraft and natural magic also classify their magical operations within these four elements, which have energetic characteristics quite different from each other. The Orishas, in turn, are the representation of the forces of nature, and for this very reason, plants also fit into this classification, linking humans to the divine structure of the Universe.

Oshala and all the *funfun* Orishas, responsible for the creation of the world and humankind, are classified as the element of air—*afefe* in the Yoruba language—since it is from the divine breath that Olodumare gives conscious life to the human body at birth. Fire—*inón*—is the principle of dynamism and movement and is related to the Orishas Eshu, Shango, and Aiyra. Water—*omi*—is the element of maintaining life and is identified as feminine, being related to all the female Orishas—especially Nana, Yemaya, Oshun, and Iyewa. The element of earth—*aiye* or *igbó* in the Yoruba language—is represented by the forest itself, where plants are found and which is the domain of hunters and warriors, as well as the guardian of the secrets of life and death. Thus, it is related to the Orishas Ogun, Oshossi, Babalu-aiye, Iroko, and Ossain. It is curious to note that Oya is related to all four of the elements. Being responsible for wind and storms, she is tied to the element of air; by the principle of complementarity of the pairs, being Shango's wife, she is tied to the element of fire; by her relationship with the ancestors, she is tied to the element of earth; and, being an Iyabá—a female Orisha—she is tied to the element of water.

The classification of plants relating to the elements of nature may be made, so to speak, because they belong to this or that Orisha. Other characteristics, however, are more important in this sense: a reaction to contact with the skin (causing irritation or itching, for example) characterizes the plant as associated with the fire element; its capacity to hold water (often appearing spongy, for example) characterizes its relationship to the water element; the production of sounds when shaken by the wind establishes its relationship to the air element, as does its hallucinogenic properties.

Vibration

Another essential aspect to be observed regarding the classification of plants for their magical use is the kind of vibration they carry within themselves: *gún* (excitement, activation, movement), also called hot or positive, and **èrò** (tranquility, calm, rest), also called cold or negative. All the elements of nature have plants of both vibrations in their classification, so that they may maintain the balance of the Universe.

Energy

Similarly, it is precisely this natural balance of the Universe that should be sought in the composition of the baths, fumigations, powders, and magical herbal rituals. And because they are spiritual healing agents, plants must be used *in the correct measure to remedy the imbalance of the physical or spiritual illness they propose to treat, without causing a new imbalance by being mismatched.*

It is from these two principles—vibration and energy—that the plants will be put together, or, better, combined in the preparation. Barros quotes a priest who, when teaching him about the combination of leaves, emphasizes that there are plants that are "female and male, which is why you must marry them right. Besides that, there are negative plants and positive ones, and we have to know how to put them together, to make the right combination, so as not to have complications."[12]

---

12. Barros, *A Floresta Sagrada de Ossain*, 88.

CHAPTER 4

The Sacred Harvest

The Orishas herbal witchcraft is full of mysteries, symbolism, and acts that recreate African customs in the smallest detail. Among them is the harvest of sacred leaves, which has a series of rules and rituals to be followed by its initiates. Pierre Verger, in his book *Orishas*, teaches us that:

> The harvest of the leaves must be done with extreme care, always in a wild place, where the plants grow freely. Those grown in gardens should be disregarded, because Ossain lives in the forest, in the company of **Àrònì**, a little dwarf, comparable to Saci-pererê, who has only one leg and, as is said in Brazil, permanently smokes a pipe made of snail shell stuck in a hollow stem filled with his favorite leaves. … When they [the priests] go to gather the plants for their work, they must do so in a state of purity, abstaining from sexual intercourse the night before, and going into the forest, at dawn, without speaking to anyone. Furthermore, they must be careful to leave a cash offering [coins] on the ground as soon as they arrive at the harvest site.[13]

Barros, citing Roger Bastide's *The African Religions of Brazil*, describes another rather elaborate ritual:

> The babalossain [priest] enters Ossain's kingdom by chewing on an *obi* seed [kola nut] (and perhaps also grains of African pepper). Arriving at his domain, he

---

13. Verger, *Orishas*, 122.

turns successively to each of the four cardinal points and spits out the chewed *obì* in these four directions. It thus delimits, in a symbolic way, the sacred space in which he will evolve.[14]

However, if in past years the *terreiros*—the name given to Candomblé temples—were located in rural areas, near forests, waterfalls, and open spaces close to nature, today they are in the midst of the chaos of the city, concrete, streets, and highways. With this change of scenery, many of the customs were lost or had to be reinvented out of necessity for the religion's survival in an urban environment. It is also necessary to consider the difficulty nowadays in finding wooded spaces for planting and harvesting herbs, when many of them can be easily acquired in street markets around the city or from specialized herbalists, which in no way invalidates the power of the plants to effect change—their *ashé*.

All magical herbal rituals begin when we decide which ingredients will be used and, more than that, when we go outdoors to find them, be it by entering the woods or buying them at a supermarket. To make use of the plants' magical power, more important than knowing the details of the rituals performed in Candomblé is understanding that each one of those rituals aims to sacralize the plants or animals that will be used—to make them sacred—and this begins with the personal preparation for seeking them out and handling them.

Each aspect considered and performed with focused purpose and intention strengthens the power to fulfill its magic. For this reason, I have prepared a short guide for you to turn your harvest into a sacred act:

---

14. Barros, *A Floresta Sagrada de Ossain*, 24.

- Keep your body clean by avoiding sexual relations on the day you prepare your bath or fumigation, as well as the day before.

- If you go out to harvest herbs in nature, ask Ossain for permission to enter his domain, calling him to help you find what you want and promising to take only the necessary amount for your ritual.

- If going into nature, leave some coins of current value as soon as you enter this sacred space, as a way of thanking Ossain and Eshu. If you can, also offer some honey, *cachaça* (sugarcane liquor) or another kind of spirit, and some tobacco.

- Never harvest leaves at night; after sunset and until the next day, all leaves get influenced by negative energies that may compromise your objective.

- Avoid picking herbs on the side of the road, under train tracks, or under high-voltage power lines, as they may be contaminated by pollution and chemicals that may cancel its *ashé*.

- When the needed part of a plant is the bark, do not tear it all off, just the bark of a branch or a strip perpendicular to the trunk, allowing the plant to remain alive.

Later on, we will see some more guidelines that must be observed to compose your recipes, such as the moon phase and the day of the week. Read all of them carefully and plan your rituals with these guidelines in mind from the first day on which you pick your ingredients—whether in nature or in a specialized store.

CHAPTER 5

Magical Aspects for Creating Baths & Fumigations

The magic of herbal baths and fumigations is not restricted to Orishas witchcraft. Many other traditions also use plant elements in the composition of their rituals, all linked to the observation of nature, the stars, and the seasons. Among them, European magic, Brazilian indigenous traditions and American shamanism are prominent. These cultures influenced the formation of many current religions, such as Umbanda, Hoodoo, and Wicca. Their relationship with nature, and often with the Orishas, has provided us with a wealth of knowledge and energy that should also be considered when creating our baths and fumigations and performing our rituals. However, it is important to remember that, although this knowledge serves us as magical instruments, the information is not magical in itself and must always obey the principles of activation, balance, and inequality so that it is useful to us.

Furthermore, when it comes to using the sacred power of plants, you can use these magical aspects at three different stages, combining their forces and influences to strengthen and enhance the intended results:

- When harvesting, if you go into the forest to get your ingredients
- When preparing your baths, fumigations, or magic powders—which can be used immediately or saved for future use
- When using each recipe or performing each specific ritual

The Four Elements

Air, fire, water, and earth, as we have seen, are closely related to the classification of plants and the Orishas that rule them. In addition to this relationship, Gerina Dunwich—one of the most famous witches in Europe—teaches us that "it was the Greco-Roman philosophical school known as Stoicism that connected the zodiac signs, the seasons, the colors, and all the [European] gods and goddesses to each of the four elements."[15] The four elements are also linked to the four cardinal points, each having special influences on our rituals' forces and specific objectives.

Air

The air element is related to the east cardinal point, where the sun rises, and to the spring equinox, the season of the year when life begins to germinate and flourish again. It is a male element, influencing our mind and thoughts. For these reasons, plants linked to the air element should be used mainly in rituals that seek to activate our creativity, new beginnings, travel, organization of thoughts and practical life, writing and communication, and the activation of spiritual sensitivity. Its symbol animals are the eagle and the falcon.

Fire

The fire element is related to the south cardinal point, representing light and technology, and to the summer solstice, when temperatures increase and the power of life is strengthened in our hearts. It is a male element, influencing sexuality and ardent passions, physical and spiritual protection, courage, and success. Additionally, fire also acts as a catalyst to destroy negative feelings such as anger, jealousy, and envy. Its animal symbol is the lion.

---

15. Gerina Dunwich, *Desvendando a Arte dos Feitiços: Como Criar e Realizar Feitiços Eficazes*, trans. Márcia Frazão (Rio de Janeiro: Bertrand Brasil, 2003), 20. Translated from the Portuguese.

Water

The water element is related to the west cardinal point and represents the soul, pregnancy, love, and the autumn equinox, the moment when life is moving toward the end of its natural cycle. It is a female element that influences clairvoyance and intuition, emotional balance, children, love, and all kinds of relationships. Its animal symbols are the fish and the seahorse.

Earth

The earth element is related to the north cardinal point and represents the physical body and the generation of life, being the Great Mother of the Universe, and to the winter solstice, the time when everything returns to its origin in order to be reborn and fulfill the natural cycle of life. It is a female element that influences protection and healing, fertility and pregnancy, and everything related to prosperity, abundance, career, and business. Its animal symbols are the bull and the bear.

The Days of the Week

Sunday

Ruled by Olodumare, Orunmila, and Olorun, lords of creation and universal knowledge, alongside Nana, Oshalufan, Obatala, and all the *funfun* Orishas, Sunday favors objectives related to learning and studies; calm, peace, and the generation of new fruits; longevity and older people; and meditation and reflection.

Monday

Ruled by the Orishas Eshu and Babaluaiye, Monday favors objectives related to health, the healing of physical and spiritual ills, and medicine; communication, sexuality, and pleasure; the start of new projects; and also the resolution of conflicts and competitions.

Tuesday

Ruled by the Orishas Ogun and Oshumare, Tuesday favors objectives related to the opening of paths and progress, work and career, restarting or resetting, transmutations and changes, and courage, physical strength, war, and battles.

Wednesday

Ruled by the Orishas Shango, Oya, and Obba, Wednesday favors objectives related to legal matters, documents, and papers; loyalty, vitality, and sensuality; authority, writing, and reason; and also politics and leadership issues.

Thursday

Ruled by the Orishas Oshossi, Ossain, and Logunede, Thursday favors objectives related to growth, prosperity, and material inheritances and gains; hunting and the conquest of goals; childhood and children; partnerships and friendships; and logic, learning, and studies.

Friday

Ruled by the Orishas Oshala and Oshoguian, Friday favors objectives related to spirituality, peace, and tranquility; the strengthening of faith and perseverance; and divine powers and the purification of the body and soul.

Saturday

Ruled by all female Orishas, especially Oshun, Yemaya, Iyewa, and Nana, Saturday favors objectives related to family, pregnancy, and fertility; love and relationships; arts and creativity; and dreams and intuition.

The Moon and Its Phases

Since ancient times, the phases of the moon have been influencing human life and rituals—be they magical rituals or daily rituals. It is no wonder that many people use the lunar calendar to make important decisions in their lives, such as harvesting, cutting their hair, or starting a business. Fishermen and peasants, for example, did not know the magical influences of the phases of the moon, but even so, in using them they always knew the best period for one or another activity in the countryside. Incidentally, the moon has a particular influence on women and their monthly periods. For this reason, it is considered a deity in several magical traditions precisely because it represents the different faces of the Sacred Feminine: the maiden, the mother, the crone, and the warrior are reflected and personified in each lunar cycle.

In Roma magic, as well as in Candomblé and African herbal magic, it is no different: the influence of the moon is often considered to determine the best time to perform a certain type of ritual, bath, or fumigation, depending on the goals we want to achieve. For rituals of praise to Ori, for example, our personal Orisha, or in *ebós*, the magical rituals that seek prosperity and the opening of paths, it is essential to consider the way the moon is positioned in the sky.

It's undeniable: magic and folk wisdom mix when we talk about the ways each phase of the moon influences and interferes with our rituals, our daily lives, and even our moods. So … what are, after all, the powers and objectives that must be worked on in each one of the phases?

Waxing Moon

This is the phase in which the moon comes out of the darkness and begins to grow, illuminating the sky. Therefore, it is favorable for rituals of growth and attraction. Rituals that aim to increase what is desired or that have to do with the birth of children; strengthening of friendships and relationships; love, sensuality, and feelings; harmonizing situations and environments; good luck; and business and prosperity should be performed during this period.

Full Moon

This is the phase when the moon is most visible and bright, reigning full in the sky. It is during this period that spiritual energies reach their peak and consolidate, vibrating more strongly. It is thus a proper time for rituals of strengthening, fulfillment, fertility, virility and sexuality, communication, radiance, success and visibility, partnerships and signing contracts, happiness, courage and fortitude, conquest and mastery, defining love situations, and the performing of marriages.

Waning Moon

This is the phase in which the moon's brightness decreases until it disappears and stays hidden for a few days. It is a favorable moment for the closure of everything that is no longer necessary or desired, the banishment of negative energies, liberation and finalization, the reversal of unwanted situations, healing (in the sense of eliminating illness), symbolic death and resurrection, maturity, and ancestral wisdom.

New Moon

This is the phase in which the moon is not visible in the sky, when it is preparing to be reborn in its new cycle. Therefore, it is a period of energetic instability, full of mysteries and insecurities, a time of darkness and of reclusion and seclusion, favorable for meditation and self-knowledge.

Void Moon

There are days when all we need—or at least all we'd like—is to stop, isn't that right? Turning off the cell phone, getting off of social media, forgetting about email, and looking inside ourselves ... Staying a little longer in bed, or maybe stretching out on the couch a little, as if there were no worries and commitments out there. A moment to recharge your energies, to not think about anything, and at the same time, to refresh the plans and projects that you will be carrying out in the days to come ...

In magic, this moment also exists! The void moon—also called the out-of-course moon—happens every two or three days, whenever the moon completes its last aspect in any of the signs of the zodiac, until the moment when it enters the next sign. This period can last for a few minutes or even hours, and during this time, magical works and rituals must be avoided entirely, at the risk of having their objectives nullified, as in this period everything that is initiated tends to be uncertain and is subject to mistakes and frustration.

The first astrologer to popularize the void moon was the American Al Morrison, who observed that all actions taken while the moon is out of its course fail for some reason in their planned or intended results. It is a period of spiritual and energetic withdrawal, which must be used for self-observation and planning new goals. During the void moon phase, people in general tend to seem disconnected from reality, as if they were pulled into themselves, becoming less rational and making it difficult to have good judgment and clarity in making decisions. For this reason, we should avoid taking any important and decisive action for our lives, for example:

- Starting relationships
- Signing agreements
- Buying or selling goods such as cars and real estate

- Releasing products or starting a new business
- Opening shows, plays, or exhibitions
- Participating in job interviews
- Starting a new career
- Having surgeries or medical interventions—except emergency ones
- Taking long trips
- Having conversations to resolve relationships
- Trying out new processes or procedures in any area
- Taking tests or exams
- Formalizing or contracting medium- and long-term business deals

Still, the void moon periods have their advantages, as they connect us in a particular way to our inner self. Thus, these moments are suitable for creative leisure, for continuing what is already in progress, for the relaxation of the body and soul, and for meditation and reflection. In short, the void moons favor the subjective issues of the soul over the objective issues of matter. The days and times of the void moons vary each year and are widely publicized by astrologers around the world.

Is the Moon Void Today?
On my website you will find an article dedicated entirely to explaining what the void moon is, what its restrictions are, and what its advantages are. Additionally, you can also find the void moon table for the current year. Just access the following link: www.diegodeoxossi.com.br/void-moon.

How to Find the Moon Phase Without a Calendar
As we have seen, the moon phases are one of the most important aspects in the creation of your baths and fumigations and in

the performance of your magic rituals. However, we often need to find out which phase the moon is in and have no way of using a printed calendar or the internet or a cell phone. How do you know which phase the moon is in without looking at a calendar? Well, there are some simple ways:

By Its Visibility During the Day
If, when looking at the sky during the day, the moon is visible in the afternoon, it is in a waxing phase. On the contrary, if it appears in the morning, it is in a waning phase.

By the Cardinal Points
This is a bit more complicated, because you need to know in which direction the sun rises and sets from your observation point, and it is valid for observations in both hemispheres of the earth. If the moon appears in the west before midnight (where the sun sets), it is in a waxing phase. However, if after midnight it is visible in the east (where the sun rises), it is in a waning phase.

By Its Shape
Another way to identify what phase the moon is in is by observing its shape in the sky. In the Northern Hemisphere, above the equator, if the moon appears in the shape of the letter D, it means that it is in the waxing phase. If, on the other hand, the shape of the moon resembles the letter C, it means that it is in the waning phase. Now, if it's glowing round and white, you can bet it's a full moon, and if it's dark, as if it were wearing a black veil, it's a new moon! This method, however, only applies to the Northern Hemisphere. In the Southern Hemisphere, the moon's appearance is reversed, and, therefore, when having the shape of the letter D it is waning, while the shape of the letter C means it is waxing.

Ah! A curiosity: in the regions closest to the equator, this rule of the moon's shape does not apply! Do you know why? Because in these regions the moon appears lying down, as if it were a boat sailing in the sky (or upside down, like an arch, depending on the phase it is in).

The Planets and Magic

The Key of Solomon is a grimoire (the name given to a book that gathers recipes and secrets of magic) attributed to the mythological King Solomon, but its origin was probably in the Middle Ages. *The Key of Solomon* contains a collection of thirty-six pentacles—symbols that have magical or esoteric meanings—that enable a connection between the physical and spiritual planes. The principles described in this text are still considered a reference for several magic scholars, including renowned authors such as the occultists Cornelius Agrippa, Francis Barrett, Eliphas Levi, and Papus. In it, King Solomon organizes the seven planets of traditional astrology and defines their powers and areas of influence in a very detailed way. Of course King Solomon has nothing to do with African Orishas, but taking into consideration his lessons on each day of the week and its energy resemblances, we can define which Orishas are related to this or that energy, as you'll see next.

Sun

The days and hours of the sun are recommended for the work to achieve wealth, fortune, and personal benefits; they dissolve hostile feelings and help friendships and social relationships; ambition, authority, fame, and prominent positions are their domain. They are related to the Orishas Oshossi, Oshun, Logunede, and Oshumare.

Venus

Venus's days and hours are linked to love, beauty, and sensuality; new friendships, trips, vacations, and all matters involving pleasure and the fine arts are also strengthened by their energies, as are arts, creativity, and youth. They are related to the Orishas Oshun, Oshossi, and Iyewa.

Mercury

Mercury's days and hours are related to the development of intelligence, studies, and documents; physical and occult sciences; inspiration and spiritual sensitivity; commerce and business in general; advice and communication; speed and the movement of that which is stagnant; and the healing of body, mind, and soul. They are related to the Orishas Eshu and Ossain.

Moon

The moon's days and hours are recommended for love spells, reconciliation, travel, and diplomacy; secrets and truths; hidden messages; attracting people and situations that seem far away; fertility, generation, and growth; and motherhood and feminine powers. They are related to the Orishas Oshun, Oya, and Iyewa.

Saturn

Saturn's days and hours are favorable to success and failure in business and professional paths; they favor possessions, goods, abundance, and prosperity; they also bring destruction, physical and symbolic death, and hate and discord; they are linked to the closing of cycles, wills, ancestry, and longevity. They are related to the Orishas Oshalufan, Nana, and Babaluaiye.

Jupiter

Jupiter's days and hours are excellent for the work of honor and wealth; friendships; health and achieving goals; financial and business matters; foreign relations; new jobs and professional changes; good luck; political power; and legal and bureaucratic matters. They are related to the Orishas Shango and Oya.

Mars

Mars's days and hours are related to the energy of war and battles, courage, the defeat of enemies and vexing situations, cruelty, breaking demands and spells, exorcisms and discharges, and legal matters and disputes. They are related to the Orishas Ogun, Obba, Oya, and Oshoguian.

Planetary Hours

Besides the elements of nature, the days of the week, and the phases of the moon, another important aspect to be considered is planetary hours, widely used by many traditions of ceremonial magic since Ancient times, which from their regency can enhance with different energies each of our ritual's purposes. The influences of planetary hours are based on the seven planets of traditional astrology: the Sun, Venus, Mercury, the Moon, Saturn, Jupiter, and Mars. According to Stewart Farras, in his book *What Witches Do*, "the first hour following sunrise is governed by the ruling planet of the day, while the subsequent hours are governed by each of the other stars ... successively and in a rotating order."[16]

It is important to note this statement, because planetary hours are not calculated according to normal clock time; rather, they are based on the exact time of sunrise and sunset, which will define the day and night periods and the duration of each planetary hour. For this reason, depending on the season of the year and the region where you live, planetary hours may be slightly more or slightly less than the usual sixty minutes. Similarly, the period considered "day" does not refer to the first hour of the morning, but to the first planetary hour from the time of sunrise; likewise, the first hour of the night period will be considered to be from the exact minute of sunset.

---

16. Quoted in Dunwich, *Desvendando a Arte dos Feitiços*, 63.

To calculate the planetary hours for a given day, the following steps must be followed: (1) having obtained the exact times of sunrise and sunset, the time in minutes between one and the other must be calculated; (2) divide this total amount of minutes by 12; (3) the number that results will be the length of each planetary hour on the given day. The first hour of the day will then correspond to the planet ruling the day of the week:

- The **Sun** rules **Sunday**.
- The **Moon** rules **Monday**.
- **Mars** rules **Tuesday**.
- **Mercury** rules **Wednesday**.
- **Jupiter** rules **Thursday**.
- **Venus** rules **Friday**.
- **Saturn** rules **Saturday**.

The other planetary hours will begin, then, at the exact minute that the previous one ends, and they will be governed by the planet immediately following the regent of the previous hour, according to this sequence: (1) the Sun, (2) Venus, (3) Mercury, (4) the Moon, (5) Saturn, (6) Jupiter, and (7) Mars. Gerina Dunwich further teaches us that "the dividing minute between two planetary hours is known as the cusp. Because of the unstable energy that occurs with the contact between two different planetary influences, this moment is not recommended to perform magical works."[17]

To better understand how to calculate planetary hours, observe the following example: the sunrise of January 1, 2016, a Friday, occurred at 05:23, and the sunset occurred at 18:57. Thus, the total amount of time between them is 814 minutes, which, divided by 12, totals 68 minutes for each planetary hour. Thus, the first planetary hour of January 1, 2016, starts at 5:23 a.m. and ends 68 minutes

17. Dunwich, *Desvendando a Arte dos Feitiços*, 65.

later, at 6:31 a.m., being ruled by Venus, which is the ruling planet of Friday. The second hour of the day will then run from 6:31 a.m. until 7:39 a.m., being ruled by Mercury. The third hour, from 7:39 a.m. until 8:47 a.m., will be ruled by the Moon, and so on.

At the end of this period, the calculation for the planetary hours of the night should be done in the same way. Consider the time between sunset of the current day and sunrise of the next day, following the same sequence of regencies. To facilitate the understanding and identification of the planetary hours, the following tables present the order of regencies for each day of the week, in the both day and night periods.

Planetary Hours of the Day (from sunrise to sunset) and Night (from sunset to sunrise)

Sunday	
Day	Night
1. Sun	1. Jupiter
2. Venus	2. Mars
3. Mercury	3. Sun
4. Moon	4. Venus
5. Saturn	5. Mercury
6. Jupiter	6. Moon
7. Mars	7. Saturn
8. Sun	8. Jupiter
9. Venus	9. Mars
10. Mercury	10. Sun
11. Moon	11. Venus
12. Saturn	12. Mercury

Monday

Day	Night
1. Moon	1. Venus
2. Saturn	2. Mercury
3. Jupiter	3. Moon
4. Mars	4. Saturn
5. Sun	5. Jupiter
6. Venus	6. Mars
7. Mercury	7. Sun
8. Moon	8. Venus
9. Saturn	9. Mercury
10. Jupiter	10. Moon
11. Mars	11. Saturn
12. Sun	12. Jupiter

Tuesday

Day	Night
1. Mars	1. Saturn
2. Sun	2. Jupiter
3. Venus	3. Mars
4. Mercury	4. Sun
5. Moon	5. Venus
6. Saturn	6. Mercury
7. Jupiter	7. Moon
8. Mars	8. Saturn
9. Sun	9. Jupiter
10. Venus	10. Mars
11. Mercury	11. Sun
12. Moon	12. Venus

Wednesday	
Day	*Night*
1. Mercury	1. Sun
2. Moon	2. Venus
3. Saturn	3. Mercury
4. Jupiter	4. Moon
5. Mars	5. Saturn
6. Sun	6. Jupiter
7. Venus	7. Mars
8. Mercury	8. Sun
9. Moon	9. Venus
10. Saturn	10. Mercury
11. Jupiter	11. Moon
12. Mars	12. Saturn

Thursday	
Day	*Night*
1. Jupiter	1. Moon
2. Mars	2. Saturn
3. Sun	3. Jupiter
4. Venus	4. Mars
5. Mercury	5. Sun
6. Moon	6. Venus
7. Saturn	7. Mercury
8. Jupiter	8. Moon
9. Mars	9. Saturn
10. Sun	10. Jupiter
11. Venus	11. Mars
12. Mercury	12. Sun

Friday

Day	Night
1. Venus	1. Mars
2. Mercury	2. Sun
3. Moon	3. Venus
4. Saturn	4. Mercury
5. Jupiter	5. Moon
6. Mars	6. Saturn
7. Sun	7. Jupiter
8. Venus	8. Mars
9. Mercury	9. Sun
10. Moon	10. Venus
11. Saturn	11. Mercury
12. Jupiter	12. Moon

Saturday

Day	Night
1. Saturn	1. Mercury
2. Jupiter	2. Moon
3. Mars	3. Saturn
4. Sun	4. Jupiter
5. Venus	5. Mars
6. Mercury	6. Sun
7. Moon	7. Venus
8. Saturn	8. Mercury
9. Jupiter	9. Moon
10. Mars	10. Saturn
11. Sun	11. Jupiter
12. Venus	12. Mars

CHAPTER 6

Magic in Practice

I t's time to get your hands on the ground—or better, on the leaves! To do this, you need to understand the best way to use them, and this will depend on your objective. The power of the plants can be awakened and used for several purposes, such as spiritual cleansing, love, or the opening of paths, for example. In the same way, the rituals can be applied in different ways: to yourself, to other people, to your home or workplace, and even to people and places that are difficult to reach. For every different application there will be a different way of using African herbal witchcraft: baths, fumigations, soaps, powders, or shamanic sticks. Let's take a look at each one of them…

Fumigations

Smokings and fumigations are, perhaps, the best-known way to use sacred leaves. They are commonly found in Santeria shops and esoteric stores in the form of dry leaves, tablets, or incense sticks. The principle of using fumigations is the smoke created by burning previously dried elements, formed, therefore, by the dominance of the earth element over the fire element, with the predominance of fire. For this reason, fumigation has an active vibration and is always used to move the desired energies.

Due to its versatility, the smoke from fumigations can expand throughout the environment and permeate the space as a whole, cleaning and energizing even the hard-to-reach corners, walls, and furniture, as well as objects that cannot get in touch with the water of baths, for example. As with powders, which we will see below, the energy of fumigation can be directed according to its objective—from the inside out, to expel the harmful energies, and from the outside in, to attract what you want.

Another way of directing the smoke's energy is by choosing the direction you move in when distributing it: to start, attract, or move, this must be done in a counterclockwise direction from the starting point, moving from right to left; to end, repel, or ban, it must be done clockwise, moving from left to right.

It is important to remember that the more smoke there is, the more powerful the application of the fumigation will be. Therefore, the leaves used in these recipes must be very dry and preferably will have been dehydrated naturally by exposure to the sun. Besides using new leaves and drying them out, you can also use what is left of leaves you have prepared as a bath, drying them in the sun, to create your fumigations.

Shamanic Sticks

As we have already seen, the best-known forms of fumigation are the burning of dried leaves on hot coals or incense tablets. However, there is another way that, in my opinion, is more complete and more beautiful: burning herbal sticks or shamanic sticks. Like other types of baths and fumigations, shamanic sticks can be created in various forms and combinations of herbs, flowers, and seeds—always fresh and without going through the drying process—bound in a cylindrical shape and tied with threads of silk or cotton, or even vines or branch leaves. They are usually between 10 and 30 centimeters long, and what I love most about them is that, in addition to the magical use of smoke during the burning of the herbs, they also have other special functions.

The first of these is aesthetic: you can include various ingredients in creating your stick to make it visually beautiful and use it as a decorative element in your home or work, like a floral arrangement. Also, while waiting for its ingredients to dry completely, shamanic sticks can be hung on your house's doors or windows, where they will serve as amulets and talismans to attract good energies and ward off negative ones.

Powders

Powders are another way of using sun-dried leaves, and for that they need to be crushed and sifted until they are very fine. In some cases, a powder's ingredients must also be roasted; in others, roasting cancels the recipe's power. Its principle of use is the powder itself, being formed by the dominance of the earth element over the air element, with the predominance of air.

Powders can be used in several ways, and generally their use aims to apply their magic on places or people without their noticing, or even on places and objects in which we want to maintain the powder's vibration continuously. To do this, they can be blown, sprinkled, or mixed in drinks and food as if they were spices. Powders of great power usually involve elaborate rituals for their preparation, as they need to concentrate their magic in small portions, even in almost imperceptible pinches. This, however, does not mean that powders with simple preparations have less effect—what needs to be taken into account at the end of it all is where or on whom you will apply them, since the primary purpose of powders is to be imperceptible to the naked eye.

Baths

Herbal baths are the most direct way to use the power of leaves. They are prepared for application on the body or to wash the places where and objects on which you wish to apply their magic. However, as you have already learned, each leaf and each magical ingredient has a distinct vibration. In the case of baths, it is very important to pay attention to your recipe's vibration, considering all the elements used in its composition. This is because its vibration will determine the correct way to take it: from head to toe or from the neck down.

Our head—the *Ori* of African spiritual traditions—is the main energy point of the body; it is the place of connection with the sacred, and also of physical and spiritual balance. For this reason, baths of active vibration, made up of red or hot leaves or ingredients, should only be taken from head to toe if you are absolutely sure of the vibration of your recipe and, especially, if you are sure that the ingredients used do not counteract the energies of your ruling Orisha.

When using magic baths, the important thing is to extract the plants' juice, which can be obtained in two ways: by boiling or simmering them in water, like a tea, or by mashing the ingredients with your hands or in a pestle and then macerating or soaking them. Ah! Even though the preparation of magic herbal baths is mostly done with cold water, when taking them—whether boiled or macerated—you can add hot water or even water from the shower to warm it up.

Boiled

Boiled baths are generally of active vibration. They move, attract, accelerate, and warm up our goals. They are formed with the dominance of the earth element over the water element, with the predominance of earth, and for this reason, they are mainly related to male Orishas such as Eshu, Ogun, Oshossi, Omolu, and Shango, or to female Orishas with hot temperaments, such as Oshun, Iansã, and Obba. Their preparation is very similar to that of a tea: the leaves and ingredients are placed in boiling water for about five to ten minutes, and after that time, turn off the heat and steep the stewed leaves in the hot water until it cools.

Macerated

Macerated baths, generally speaking, are of passive vibration. They calm down, harmonize, and rebalance the energies of our goals. Made by the dominance of the earth element over the water element, with the predominance of water, they are mainly related to all female Orishas and to Oshala, the god of creation. This type of bath is prepared by direct manipulation of the ingredients, which must be mashed by hand or with a pestle, mixed in fresh water, and then strained, using the water resulting from this mixture as a bath. Macerated baths can commonly be taken from head to toe.

The Dangers of the Coarse Salt Bath

In all magic traditions—whether Roma magic, Wicca, natural magic, or African magic—coarse salt is a magical element that catalyzes positive and negative energies, serving as a powerful element to ward off and neutralize all types of energies. One example of its proper use is that, since ancient times, salt circles have been used as protection against demons and evil spirits, as well as against envy, the evil eye, and curses. As another example, on the other hand, in the Candomblé tradition the act of spilling coarse salt on the floor of a house is a seriously ill omen and can, as we say, "burn its floor"—that is, it can negate all the people and energies that are present there, regardless of what they are!

Due to this contrast, coarse salt baths are extremely dangerous and should not be taken without precautions! Coarse salt drains all the energy, whatever it is, and even when mixed with other ingredients, it eliminates all the other herbs' energetic potential and therefore cancels the positive effect of any potion or magic recipe. Furthermore, it acts as a high-powered "astral cleaner" and leaves us vulnerable to any energy that comes along right after using this bath.

That is why, even though the coarse salt bath is very popular, I never recommend it for people who come to me for rituals and counseling; after all, there are several other magical ingredients that can be used for spiritual cleansing. However, if you really wish to use it or have been instructed to do so, remember to always take a second bath immediately after it, one very well prepared and grounded with herbs for protection and energizing! Another important tip: whenever you're going to take an herbal bath, whatever your goal, replace ordinary soap with African black soap, as we'll learn about now.

African Black Soap

Traditionally, in Candomblé, the use of root, seed, and plant preparations to purify and energize the human body or liturgical instruments is preceded by a hygienic bath in which the whole body is washed normally and, unless otherwise indicated, rinsed with clean water. However, the difference between these and ordinary day-to-day baths lies in the fact that the magic begins exactly at this very moment.

First of all, the use of pure water is a real and symbolic form of cleansing and purification of the ritual object in question. A life-giving element, water has a sacred character within the religions of African origin, being present in practically all rituals. It is not for nothing that with it, animals are washed before sacrifice, initiates' heads are wet with water as a sign of blessing, and the clay bottles that are always kept at the Orishas' shrines are filled up with it, as its material represents a clear reference to the human body, its organic composition, and its (re)approximation with the sacred.

The second difference comes in replacing ordinary soap with African black soap—also called *Dudu Ose*—a pasty, dark-colored soap sold in all the large markets along the Atlantic coast of Africa. (Thus, its name in Portuguese is *sabão-da-costa*, or "coast soap.") Imported from Africa to Brazil since 1620, its main producers at the time it was first introduced were Ghana, Cameroon, Nigeria, Togo, and the former Dahomey—currently the Republic of Benin. African black soap used to be brought from Africa in the holds of slave ships, sometimes by enslaved people themselves, but mostly by their traffickers, who saw soap's commercialization as another way of producing wealth. Even so, it was only in the 1970s, in Rio de Janeiro, that African black soap became popular. Due to the recognition of its medicinal and magical properties, its demand and consequent supply grew in the shops that sell religious articles—which, since then, has contributed to the massive and legalized import of the product.

Made of a mixture of animal fat and plant paste, the standard African black soap is energetically formed by the union of the four elements of nature—earth, fire, water, and air—and can be used as a base ingredient for different forms of preparations and applications. Depending on the magic or therapeutic recipe for which it is recommended, it can be mixed with fresh or dried herbs, several spices, oils, minerals, and a myriad of other ingredients.

In general, the preparation of rituals that use African black soap takes place in the same way as in any other case: the proper ingredients are chosen, as are the day of the week, the planetary hour, and the favorable moon phase, and then, with the use of the hands or a pestle, everything is homogeneously mixed into the base paste. As with fumigations, baths, and powders made with sacred plants, your spells must observe the rules of the combination and energetic balance of their ingredients. Further, it is important to remember that, in the same way, the powers of African black soap also need to be activated through the correct incantations for its magical effects to achieve the desired goals, as we will see in the chapters that follow.

Waji: The African Indigo

Among the various ingredients used in Candomblé recipes, the so-called *ashé* powders are perhaps the most prominent. *Efun, Osun,* and *Waji* are their names, and each of them has broad uses and meanings, being indispensable in almost all rituals of cleansing and spiritual strengthening. These *ashé* powders also represent a form of protection against the evil forces of the three main *Iyami Àjé*—ancestral witches—preventing them from landing on people's spiritual bodies and negatively influencing their paths. The combination of these powders also aims to unite the whole spiritual force, or *ashé*, transmitted to the novice during the rites of initiation.

Of all of them, *Waji* is the most well known and widespread outside of the terreiros, being widely recommended for the energetic cleansing of homes, businesses, and people. *Waji* is a type of blue powder resulting from the mixture of minerals whose composition is sodium, aluminum, and silicate. A symbol of idealization and transformation, it represents the night and movement, or the way out of stagnation, and it aims to protect against all spiritual, material, and psychic evils.

Nowadays, it is possible to find African *Waji* easily in specialized stores; however, until recently, this ingredient was commonly substituted with indigo powder—which is why we can consider it to be "the African indigo"—and, of course, you can replace the original African ingredient with the standard indigo powder found in stores.

In our moments of depression and sorrow, while living in places of constant conflict, we might easily become targets of these disincarnated spirits. They stick to doorways, to the neck and the back (giving people a feeling of "weight on their shoulders"), and to cold and damp places like bathrooms and warehouses, especially in that infamous room at the back of the house full of old things of no more use to the people living there. Cleansing rituals with *Waji* bring light to spiritual darkness, moving away low-vibration spirits and dispersing any negative energies that, over time, accumulate in all corners of an environment, leaving the space with bad and low energy.

Further, spiritual cleansing rituals with *Waji*, aside from serving as a powerful defense against astral negativities, also awaken courage and willpower in people, bringing peace and harmony to their paths so that they are able to pursue their greatest goals with a calm head and a heart focused on victory. Also, scientific studies have proven the medicinal efficiency of indigo as well as its antioxidant and anti-inflammatory properties, which may be useful in the treatment of intestinal diseases such as ulcerative colitis and Crohn's disease.

In the herbal grimoire at the end of this book, when we talk about the magic recipes you can make at home, I will teach you a famous, powerful, and influential energy cleansing ritual: the Blue Ritual.

CHAPTER 7

Many Names, Many Powers

B esides being the sacred place in which to worship the Orishas, Candomblé temples are spaces for preserving the ancestral memory of its participants, who reproduce the African family structure in its most intimate aspects, "based on mythical kinship, the principle of seniority and religious initiation."[18] This "parallel reality" creates in its members a singular religious identity, loaded with symbolism originating from the Africans who experienced the conditions of slavery and resisted by adapting to their environment in order to find local elements that would guarantee them the maintenance of their dignity.

Perhaps the most symbolic of these aspects is language. The rituals, prayers, and songs of the religion of the Orishas are, to this day, performed in an ancient form of Yoruba, one that is liturgical, almost dialectical. Candomblé members know the words and their meanings in this context, but they do not always know their literal translation, and even less often do they know how to use them in new textual formations. Nevertheless, this same language has served to name its members, who are rebaptized during the initiation rites, and to designate objects, situations, and emotions, as well as, of course, to identify the plant species used in their potions, baths, fumigations, and rituals.

In the magical use of plants, the Yoruban or liturgical name, instead of the scientific name or the common name of the species, has a much greater purpose than the mere preservation of memory and religious tradition. These names carry profound symbolism and meanings that, citing Claude Levi-Strauss, "are

---

18. Barros, *A Floresta Sagrada de Ossain*, 13.

an integral part of systems treated by us as codes: ways of fixing meanings, transposing them into terms of other meanings."[19] This means that Yoruban names serve not only to identify the plants, but also to define other aspects such as their function, their magical classification, and their healing powers, as Barros explains:

> The liturgical name [of a plant], besides containing information related to its use, constitutes a clarifying element of the cognitive system, since it can inform the singular aspects that involve its use, and refer to the power of the word as a facilitator of *ashé*. *Some plants have multiple names, each related to a certain type of utility.*
>
> Therefore, calling the plant by its proper name means guaranteeing the purpose for which it is intended. ... Another case is when several plants, that is, different species, receive a single liturgical denomination [because they fulfill the same function].[20]

Barros's explanation makes quite clear the major function of using the Yoruban names of plants in order to reaffirm the desired magical objective and, once again, makes it explicit that the classification system of these species is subjective but quite functional. This classification by magical-medicinal function, for that matter, is similar to the concept of classification by botanical family found in the traditional taxonomic system. In the next chapter, we will study this matter a little better, learning how to use the common name of plants in our enchantments while loading them with the necessary *ashé* to fulfill the magical objectives of our baths and fumigations. The examples below were

---

19. Quoted in Barros, *A Floresta Sagrada de Ossain*, 9.
20. Barros, *A Floresta Sagrada de Ossain*, 57; my emphasis.

translated by me from Pierre Verger's book *Ewé*, one of the largest studies on the use of plants in African religions, to illustrate the multiplicity of names and functions.[21]

Several Plants, One Single Name

Amùjé (literally "Stop Blood") is called *Amùjè Nlá* ("Stop Blood Large") in the case of *Harungana madagascariensis* (haronga or dragon's blood tree), in the family Rhizophoraceae, and *Amùjè Wéwé* ("Stop Blood Small") in the case of *Byrsocarpus coccineus* and *Cnestis longiflora*, both from the family Connaraceae; these are plants with coagulating properties.

Bùjé is the name given to plants that are used in preparations for tattoos and hair dyes, classified as *Morelia senegalensis*, family Rubiaceae; *Rothmannia whiffieldii*, family Rubiaceae; *Rothmania longiflora*, family Rubiaceae; *Keetia leucantha*, family Rubiaceae; and *Sorindeia warneckei*, family Anacardiaceae.

Dágunró ("Stop War") is the name given to spiny or thorny plants belonging to three different families: *Dágunró Gogoro* for the *Acanthospermum hispidum*, family Compositae (bristly starbur); *Dágunró Kékeré* for the *Alternanthera pungens*, family Amaranthaceae (khaki weed); and *Dágunró Nlá* for the *Tribulus terrestris*, family Zygophyllaceae (puncture vine).

Several Names, One Single Plant

Flabellaria paniculata, family Malpighiaceae, has three names:

1. *Àjídèrè*, which means "awakening-guarantee-fortune," used in rituals to obtain honor and glory, àwúre olá níní, with the incantation *"Ewè àjídèrè di ire gbogbo*

---

21. Pierre Fatumbi Verger, *Ewé: The Use of Plants in Yoruba Society* (São Paulo: Companhia das Letras, 1995), 23.

wá," or "Awakening-guarantee-fortune leaf, bring me good things."

2. *Àpònkólo*, used in rituals to gain virility, *aremo*, with the incantation *"Àpònkólo kó omo wáyé,"* or *"Àpònkólo* gathers children together so they can come into the world."

3. *Lagbólagbó*, used in good-luck rituals, *àwúre oríire*, with the incantation *"Lagbólagbó* open the paths of good luck for me."

Ipomoea hederifolia, family Convolvulaceae (scarlet creeper or scarlet morning glory), has two different names for the same purpose:

1. *Etí ológbò*, "cat's ear," because of its shape, is used in rituals to acquire money, àwúre owó, with the incantation *"Etí ológbò l'ó ní é máa gb'ówó wá,"* or "Cat's ear said you would give me money." It can be used to protect against death, *idáàbòbò l'ówó ikú*, with the incantation *"Etí ológbò l'ó ní k'ó gbó,"* or "Cat's ear said you must grow old (not die)"; or it can also mean to be loved by people, àwúre iférán ènìyàn, with the incantation *"Etí ológbò l'ó ní gbogbo yín féràn mi,"* or "Cat's ear said that everyone should love me."

2. *Kawó kawó*, "count-money," is used in two rituals for acquiring money, àwúre owó, with the incantations *"Kawó kawó ò ní jí kí ó má kawó,"* or "Count-money said I will really count money," and *"Kawó kawó kìí k'ó má kawó,"* or "Count-money doesn't wake up without counting money."

CHAPTER 8

Orin Ewé: Singing to Enchant

I n religions of African origin, it is believed that every natural element, every ingredient used in rituals, every leaf, and every living thing carries within itself a portion of the Divine, a transforming force within itself. This force, called *ashé*, is what moves life and the Universe, powering our purposes and making our wishes come true, manifesting in the physical world what we imprint through faith in the spiritual world. This force, however, is dormant in each of these elements in their natural state. Thus, it is necessary to awaken it, transforming what was once a purely physical artifact into a sacred object—or, better said, *sacralizing* it—through the pronunciation of magical words that are imbued with power and will.

Pierre Verger, in his book *Ewé*, referring to the importance of the spoken word, states that while speech "is considered a vehicle for transmitting *ashé*, its power becomes ineffective in a written context. So, for words to have magical value, they must necessarily be spoken."[22] This issue can also be verified by looking at the *itans*, or myths, about the creation of life, in the words of Mãe Stella de Oshossi, priestess of Ilê Axé Opô Afonjá (a Candomblé temple in Salvador): "The man, who was molded with clay by Oshala, only came to life after receiving, in his ear, the divine breath [the words] from Olorun."[23] These magical words manifest out loud the wishes and intentions of the ritual that is being performed, as if they were true mantras.

---

22. Verger, *Ewé*, 30; my translation.
23. Mãe Stella de Oshossi, *Ofun* (Salvador: Assembléia Legislativa do Estado da Bahia, 2013), 31.

Since Candomblé is above all a festive religion, the best way to pronounce the words of its rituals is through singing. With this, *Orin Ewé* is the expression in the Yoruba language to define the sacred songs dedicated to awakening the power of the leaves. The *Orin Ewé* are, then, poems set to music, sacred incantations that praise, characterize, qualify, and highlight the powers and attributes of the plants that will be used—even though often the simple pronunciation of the magical name of a plant can wake it up, which shows the importance of speech in the transmission and realization of *ashé*.

In 2014, Mãe Stella released one of the most beautiful and complete works about the sacred songs that awaken this power in Candomblé rituals, entitled *O Que as Folhas Cantam (Para Quem Canta Folha)*, or *What the Leaves Sing (For Whom Sings the Leaf)*, from which I have transcribed the following examples:[24]

Ìpèsán (American Muskwood)
>*Ìpèsán ewé ára*
>*Ewé ta lóke wa àgbéso*
>
>*Ìpèsán, thunder leaf,*
>*The leaf that illuminates from above,*
>*Protect us, raise us up, lift us up!*

Ewé-idà-orísa (Snake Plant)
>*Bè le bé ni t'òbé o*
>*Akán kãn òkùn okùn bè le bé*
>
>*We beg swords to be like them, Quite powerful.*
>*So that we may quickly cut through evil and traps;*
>*For this we plead for their power!*

---

24. Mãe Stella de Oshossi, *O Que as Folhas Cantam (Para Quem Canta Folha)* (Brasília, Brazil: INCTI, 2014).

Apákò (Bamboo)

> *Pé le bé ni tó bè*
> *Apákò màko okun pé le bé*

> *A leaf that gives long life,*
> *That is firm and escapes storms.*
> *We beg the bamboo, the leaf of long life,*
> *To make us strong and vigorous.*

Look carefully at the Yoruba form and the translation of each of the examples: do you notice that the name of the leaf is not always explicit, but its function (thunder/strength, sword/cut/defense, long life/vigor) is always part of the composition? Also, in the second and third examples, pay attention to how changing a letter or syllable changes the songs' whole meanings.

Yoruba is a phonetic language, based on its words' vocal expression and intonation (different from Portuguese and English, which are based on spelling). This poetic freedom is fundamental and is widely used to create the sacred poems that awaken the leaves. In addition, the incantations are composed to be sung, literally. The melody and repetition of their verses when they are spoken are as important as the words. Keep this in your memory and follow along with me; I will explain why!

Creating Your Personal Incantation

An important issue to note is that Yoruba is the liturgical language used in most Candomblé temples, and just as it is part of the religious tradition, it is also part of an ethical and cultural tradition, serving as *an element of identity and resistance of Black people.* Due to their coexistence in the terreiros, Candomblé initiates end up developing an emotional relationship with the use of this language in their practices, even when it is not required, mixing Yoruba with Portuguese in their daily lives.

However, if you are not familiar with Yoruba, relax. There is no need to learn it to recite the *Orin Ewé* commonly known in Candomblé—instead, you can create your own incantations in English! The basic rules for composing incantations to awaken the power of the leaves are quite simple:

- Activation verb, word, or syllable
- Description of the desired objective
- Rhyme and musical cadence
- Repetition of the activation verb
- Repetition of the full incantation
- Pronunciation flexibility

The activation verb is the connection between the ingredient's name and its purpose for the ritual, a play on words, often also serving as a rhyming element. About this, Pierre Verger explains that:

> [The verb] is, generally, the same for all the leaves used, the same syllable found in their names ... or the same syllable accented differently ... The connecting element between the name of the leaves and the action desired in their invocation it is not always limited to the verb or word, but may also appear in a phrase.[25]

Verger further explains that certain leaves are sometimes added to recipes only because of their name, which favors the composition of the incantations in the way it is pronounced and complements the way the desired objective is expressed—once again highlighting *the importance of the spoken word to create the incantation*. He also teaches us that the reason for the combination of some ingredients (sometimes seemingly contradictory)

---

25. Verger, *Ewé*, 31–33; my translation.

only becomes clear at the moment when their incantations are pronounced and that, precisely for this reason, we must always consider the rituals in their entirety.

Moreover, as we have already seen, the incantations should not be simply *said*, but *sung*. For this reason, along with the activation verb, rhyme and the musical cadence become fundamental elements, and the repetition of the stanzas is composed as a way of reaffirming their intentions. By the way, the simpler it is to pronounce them, the more easily your incantation will be applied in a natural way and, thus, strengthened by your concentration and faith. I know it all might sound complicated … but let's take a look at a practical example from a well-known Brazilian lullaby that, even if you had known it growing up, you may never have realized its power:

> Rosemary, golden rosemary [Alecrim, alecrim dourado]
> Which was born in the field [Que nasceu no campo]
> Without being sown [Sem ser semeado]

It seems funny that a lullaby could have magical power, but it's true! Rosemary is one of the most versatile plants, serving as wild-card herb, and in this incantation we ask that it help us create opportunities even where we can't see them—being born without being sown. Another example:

> The Carnation fought with the Rose [O Cravo brigou com a Rosa]
> Under a balcony [Debaixo de uma sacada]
> The Carnation was wounded [O Cravo saiu ferido]
> And the Rose was torn apart [E a Rosa, despedaçada]

It seems sad, doesn't it? However, cloves, cinnamon, and rose petals are potent ingredients in baths for love and reconciliation with the beloved. And, as the main rule is *flexibility and your personal gift*, you can change the phrases and create them in a way that strengthens your goal through the words and the phrases you use.

Yoruba: The Sacred Language of the Orishas

As we have just seen, there are some basic rules for the composition of the incantations capable of awakening the sacred power of the leaves, and by following these rules, you can compose your incantations in the language you prefer. Still, Yoruba is the source language of the religion of the Orishas and for years and years, it has been used inside the terreiros during rituals and celebrations. For this reason, once you feel comfortable creating your incantations, it is entirely possible to unite both Yoruba and your native language in beautiful songs that will surely awaken and strengthen the magic of your intentions. Moreover, if you know the African language's grammar, you can venture into creating incantations purely in Yoruba.

Based on the book by Mãe Stella de Oshossi,[26] I have listed some key words and their respective meanings to help you out with this task. But pay attention to how an accent or a single letter completely changes the meanings of words!

A/Awa	We
Abà	Abundance
Àbá	Hope
Àbádà	Changes in life
Ãbò	Protection, defense
Afę́	Pleasure, delight
Afę́ré	Be cordial with pleasure

26. Oshossi, *O Que as Folhas Cantam*.

Àgbá	Maturity, adulthood
Àgbéso	That which is protected, exalted
Agidi	Stubborn person
Ahọ́n-iná	Flare
Aijìna	Without storm or punishment
Àiká	Innumerable
Aikùn	Who doesn't complain or whine
Airẹ	Free of wear
Àitẹ̀	Rectitude
Akán	Lightness, quickness
Àkọtan	Perfectly built or created
Akú	Dead
Alá/Oni	The one that owns and is the owner
Àlá	Dream, vision
Alãbo	Protector, guardian
Aló	Flaming fire
Amã	Always, habit, custom
Àmala	Stunning
Anú	Mercy, compassion
Ará/Egbẹ́	Community, social group
Ãra	Thunder
Àrira	As quick as can be
Aro	Sadness
Àroyé	Debate, discussion
Arù	Loaded baggage
Arúfin	Prisoner
Ãsà	Celebration, homage
Asà	Shield, defense
Asọ̀	Dispute, discussion
Àṣẹ	Energy, strength, power
Awá	The search
Ãwẹ̀	Fasting

Awo	Mystery, secret
Àwúre	Spell for good luck
Ayaya	Good mood
Ayọ̀	Joy, pleasure, exaltation
Ba	Hide
Bá	Find
Baba	Father, master
Bágbe	Live together
Bǎrá	Beg
Bárò	Ask for advice, advise
Bárù	Help someone carry their burden
Batì	Lean on someone
Bẹ́	Escape
Bè	Ask, beg
Bí	Be born, generate, give birth
Bò	Full or with plenty of leaves
Bò	Cover, hide
Bọ	To worship, adore
Bọ́	Feed
Bori	Overcome
Burú	Mean, sick
Dá	Stay alone, quiet
Dà	Transform
Dáni	Win a fight or dispute
Dárà	Do good deeds
Dè	Unite, combine
Di	Transform, become, enchant
Domi	Become watery
Dùn	Sweet, kind
Ejì	Rain
Ejìgbọ̀	Rain that brings prosperity
Èlé	Excess, usury

Èni	Today, courtesy
Èpe	Curse, plague
Ero	Thought, idea, plan, project
Ẹru èjé	To be a slave to an oath
Ète	Intention, proposal
Etutu	Gratification, gift, offering
Ewé	Leaf
Èwe	Young, youth
Ẹbẹ̀	Supplication
Ẹbọ	Sacrifice, offer
Ẹ̀jè	Blood
Ẹ̀jẹ́	Sworn
Ẹjọ́	Trouble, confusion
Ẹkọ̀	Courage, cheer
Ẹ̀kùn	Abundance and fullness
Ẹ̀lú	Mixture, modification
Ẹ̀mí	Life, breath, spirit
Ẹrọ	Calm
Ẹrú	Slave
Ẹ̀san	Revenge
Ẹti	Difficulty making a decision
Ẹ̀wẹ	Once again, again
Farabalè	Be modest, humble
Fẹ	To surprise
Fẹ́	Wish
Fẹ̀rẹ̀	With pleasure
Fi	Be unstable
Fitì	Put a complete stop to, close
Fon	Disembodied, dead
Fún	Under the care of
Furu	Quietly and quickly
Gbá	Clean

Gbédè	Hear and understand a language
Gbéjẹ	Stay quiet
Gbéṣè	Go ahead, take the lead
Gbẹ̀ṣẹ	Make a mistake
Gbó	Aging, maturing
Gbogbo	All
Gbọ̀	Succeed
Gún	Excitement
Ibárò	Advise, ask for advice
Ibi	Evil
Ibọ́	Food
Ibọ́lọ́wọ́	Escape, liberation, freedom
Ifà	Good luck, advantage
Ìfẹ́	Love
Igbe	Crying
Ìjì	Storm
Ìkú	Death
Ilà	Family, tribal brand
Ilé	House
Ìló	Departure, go away
Ìmí	Resistence
Ìna	Punishment
Ire	Kindness, benevolence, blessing
Iran	Descendant
Iso	Tying
Ìṣà	Downpour
Ìṣẹ́	Tiredness
Ìwa	Behavior
Ìyá	Mother
Iye	Importance, value
Iyìn	Honor, esteem
Já	Make problems, close paths

Jẹ	Get, gain
Jẹ́jẹ	Promise, swear
Jère	Win, get a reward
Jõ	Beg pardon
Jòwó	Allow
Ká	Harvest the fruit
Káfi	Give yourself to someone
Kan	Deceitful, harmful, bitter
Kán	Break, leave, divide
Kẹ́	Favor
Kẹ́	Keep calm
Ki	Importance, value
Kíyán	Quickly
Kó	Steal
Kòlófín	Person outside the law, marginal
Kóro	Whole, completely
Kòṣòro	Easy, possible, achievable
Kọ́	Learn, teach
Kọ̀	Refute
Kómọ́ra	Hold close to you
Kun	Be full, complete
Là	Be white, clean
Lakọ́	Teach to be purified
Lawó	Kind
Lãyè	Alive
Le	Able, powerful, strong
Lé	Go ahead
Lépè	Who has the power to invoke evil
Lera	Healthy, strong
Lẹ̀	Lazy
Lọ̀	Cry for lost things
Loju	Who sees all

Lọ́rọ̀	Be rich and healthy
Ma	Much
Mã	I intend, I go
Mãko	Become strong
Mèrò	Cautious and shrewd
Mi	Stir, shake, rock
Mọ́	Vanish, disappear
Mọ̀wẹ́	Be intelligent
Na	Come first
Nípa	Strong, powerful, able
Nú	Fulfill
Ogun	War, fight, challenge
Ọ̀gùn	Charm
Òjò	Rain
Òkúlẹ̀	Unproductive land
Òkún	Darkness, evil
Okun	Ability, strength
Omi	Water, juice
Òpa	Staff
Orí	Head
Óré	A long view
Orò	Customs, ritual
Ọ̀ru	Heat, energy
Oṣó	Witch
Òwerè	Fight
Owó	Money
Òye	Comprehension and wisdom
Oyin	Honey
Ọ̀bẹ́	Knives, sword
Ọdárá	Abundant, beautiful, prodigal
Ọdún	Party time, birthday
Ọfọ́	Enchantments, spells

Ọ̀gã	Master, guardian
Ọkàn	Heart, soul, spirit
Ọ̀kú	Wish long life
Ọlá	Glory, honor, dignity
Ọlọmọ	The one who cries about losing children
Ọmọ	Son
Ọrọ̀	Treasure
Ọṣẹ́	Offense
Ọtí	Alcoholic beverage
Pa	Put out fire, finish, close
Pá	Avoid fights
Pakú	Extinguish
Paradá	Disguise, hide, pretend to be
Pè	Cry
Pẹ́	For a long time, to be lasting
Pẹ̀lẹ́	Compassion for those in pain
Pẹ̀rẹ́	Made to fully open
Pọ̀	Full, sick of, filled with
Re	Hair falling out, skin changing
Ré	Initiation, to be cordial
Rere	Well-being, prosperity, and health
Ri	Find, realize, discover
Rin	Walk, wander
Rinká	Wander, walk without a destination
Ríran	Be able to predict the future
Rò	Meditate
Rọ	Thought, imagination
Rojú	Sad, ill-tempered appearance
Rorò	Austere, severe
Rọlẹ̀	Be silent
Rù	Endure, tolerate
Sàn	Make better, improve health

Ṣegùn	To make medicine
Ṣigidi	Revenge, punishment
Sínsìn	Adoration, exaltation
So	Bloom, bear fruit, produce
Ṣọpẹ́	Be grateful
Ṣòrọ	Speak
Sùn	Sleep
Ṣagidi	Be obstinate, have willpower
Ṣégum	Conquer, win, be victorous
Ṣògo	Glorify oneself
Ṣòro	Difficult
Ṣoro	Violent
Ta	Be persistent
Tán	Come to the end, finish
Tantan	Fully, completely
Tè	Venerate, respect
Ti	Take something or somebody by force
Tì	Encourage
Tináràn	Put out fire, light up, burn
Tìwatìwa	With dignity
Tó	Before
Tòri	Fiercely
Tóri	Fall into grace, be blessed
Tóto	Repentance before the Orishas
Tòju	Take care, look after
Tú	Untie
Tù	Favor, ease pain, soothe
Tutu	Joyfully, lit up
Tútù	Cold, cool, green
Wá	Divide
Wàlẹ́	Become sober from alcohol
Wára	In a hurry

Wàrawèré	Immediately
Wé	Think, plan
Wère	Foolish person
Wẹ̀	Wash, purify
Wiwi	Chat
Wò	Sunrise, clear
Wò	Observe, be careful
Wó	Dishonest
Wọn	Separate
Wú	Being grouchy
Yá	Immediate, fast
Yé	Cease, stop
Yè	Be flawless, perfectionist
Yèyè	Mom
Yẹ́	To honor
Yìn	Praise
Yọ	Rebirth, get rid of danger
Yọ̀	Be happy, become happy

CHAPTER 9

Inequality & Magical Balance

A s with everything else in the Universe, humans, animals, and plants are made of energy. It is the amount and type of energy contained in each of us that will determine our ability to carry out our daily activities, wake up in the morning, grow, run, or do anything. Similarly, it is the amount and type of energy concentrated in a bath or fumigation that will determine the strength of its realizing power and the effectiveness of it.

However, being energy, either a lack of or an excess of strength will be detrimental to our goal's success. For this reason—*and this is a very important rule!*—the correct composition of a bath is not done by combining all possible and imaginable ingredients for the same purpose at the same time. Doing that would be like building a nuclear bomb … I mean, have you ever stopped to think about why a bomb is so lethal?

The radioactive elements in a nuclear bomb—used to kill—are the same as those that allow doctors to perform X-ray exams and administer cancer treatments—used to save lives. So, it isn't the ingredients that make it deadly? The answer is no! What makes a bomb lethal is the *amount* of energy it has accumulated inside it that is discharged all in one go. Remember: above all, we are made up of the balance of energies—*and our recipes should also be like this*.

Inequality

The concept of energy balance is so important to African magic that even the cowrie-shell divination—the oracle that involves casting cowrie shells and reading them to translate the Orishas' counsel—is based on it. The sixteen shells that make up the oracle and the sixteen *Odu* they represent—the patterns of destiny that present themselves during the consultation—relate to the four cardinal points and are divided into two groups: eight female shells and eight male shells, which balance each other through complementary positive-negative pairs. Therefore, the even order 2–4–8–16 represents the stability and eternity of the Universe, constancy, continuity, and the maintenance of reality as it is. In the same way, the odd order 1–3–5–7–9, due to its inequality, is related to imbalance, instability, movement, disorder, and the ending of things and situations!

This conceptual difference of equality-inequality is reflected in the creation and performance of magical rituals. Understanding these concepts is essential for you to learn how to create your baths and fumigations properly. From this idea, the number of ingredients that will compose your recipes is determined, for example, based on the objective you want to achieve: the use of even quantities of ingredients represents a strengthening or stabilizing purpose, while odd quantities, in turn, are related to rituals to achieve changes, transformation, and an exchange between a state of equilibrium and another state. By the way, we can compare the ingredients of a magic recipe to the letters of a word: alone, they mean little, but when combined with other letters in the right way, they contribute to the formation of its meaning—which can be beautiful or offensive.

As we saw at the beginning of this book, all the physical and symbolic evils that happen to us represent diseases of the body or the spirit, and disease is not the natural state of things in the Universe. Therefore, it is the role of the magical ritual to expel this disease from our paths, to move the unfavorable energies out of the way so that they make room for the beneficial and positive energies that we desire, which will then settle down and become part of our personal nature again. This is the reason why rituals of spiritual cleansing and purification, for example, *must always be made up of an odd number of ingredients*. Through inequality, negative energies will be set in motion and driven out of our path. On the other hand, baths and incantations for love must always bear in mind the specific goal being sought: to attract a love that does not yet exist, for example, actually means to drive away loneliness, so these recipes should therefore be created with an *odd* number of elements; but when exploring a new love or when you already have a sweetheart by your side, the recipes should use an *even* number of ingredients to maintain it and fortify it.

The same rule applies for rituals of prosperity and abundance: if the goal is to attract money, for example, an *odd* number of ingredients is used (to change the current energy of scarcity and move it away); subsequently, when the desired goals are achieved, the recipes must then assume *even* numbers of ingredients, in order to make the wealth become established and to stimulate it to continue vibrating positively. This also applies to rituals and baths that seek to induce well-being, harmony, and peace. In general, these objectives aim to maintain the ideal state of things, and therefore they must be prepared in even numbers (and preferably with fresh leaves and mashed by hand or with a mortar and pestle—remember the preparation rules, too!).

Magical Balance

Just like the concept of even-or-odd ingredients, you will find the right way to combine these ingredients and balance the magical strength in your ritual by fully understanding the concept of equality-inequality. Once you have determined whether the number of ingredients will be even or odd, it's time to decide the number of active leaves (hot, male, *gún*) and calm leaves (cold, female, *èrò*) to be used so that you don't turn your recipe into a bomb—especially in recipes based on odd numbers.

Think with me: what good is a bath focused only on attracting money, for example, if it is not balanced with the right way to use that money? In such a case, the right thing to do is to balance your ritual's strength between plants that attract money and abundance and plants that attract security, personal recognition, and happiness. Another example: a bath to make yourself attractive for love must contain hot leaves and leaves for sensuality and the activation of the libido. At the same time, it must also have ingredients that attract harmony, understanding, and respect between you and your loved one. Can you imagine creating a "love bomb" that backfired, making you cling to your lover twenty-four hours a day? You can count the days before you would get sick of it; after all, "too much honey sours the mouth."

Roger Bastide, one of the greatest researchers and scholars of Candomblé traditions, tells us: "the mystical force may be too powerful for certain bodies; in that case, it is necessary to use negative herbs [calm herbs] to weaken the result, or vice versa."[27] This means that for a recipe to be considered correct and balanced, we must think about our objective's complete context. Thus, you should never use only plants and ingredients that fulfill your specific purpose, as making magic is all about understanding, manipulating, and rebalancing the energies of the Universe.

---

27. Quoted in Barros, *A Floresta Sagrada de Ossain*, 39.

How to Substitute One Leaf for Another

Sometimes we learn about a new leaf that has precisely that special property we were looking for. Or, we get a fantastic recipe from a friend, tried and tested, but it has one or more leaves that, no matter how hard we try, we can't find anywhere. So what to do then?

Well, every leaf can be replaced and resignified. This means that if we do not find exactly the one we were looking for, we can substitute it for another that is similar, based on its magical properties, without compromising the result of our ritual! It's like in the kitchen: sometimes we have a wide variety of spices available to create elaborate and complex recipes; at other times, salt, pepper, and one or two ingredients are enough to make our mouths water. In magic, two key words are fundamental and inseparable: knowledge and flexibility.

In these cases, therefore, the first thing to do is to study the missing ingredient. In which of the three fundamental colors of magic does it rank—black, red, or white? What is its element of nature, and what is its ruling Orisha? What is the physical property that is sought in it (texture, color, smell)? What is its vibration, and what is its primary energy? Answering these questions will start you on your search for a matching leaf. From there, your second search begins: which leaves, from the ones available to you, have the same characteristics and are part of the same family? Or, in the last instance, which of them can be combined with other ingredients to fulfill the same function as the original? By following this process and studying in detail the ingredient you need to replace, you will surely find a substitute leaf.

Another aspect of the classification of plant species arises when the subject is substitution: the so-called slave leaves in herbal witchcraft of the Orishas, *ewé érú* or *ewé òfá*. This concept points out that the four elements of nature and the grouping of plants that belong to each of them, as well as their vibration and their energy, obey a parent-child hierarchy, each being "governed" by the main plant. When looking for a substitute plant following one of these aspects—element of nature, energy, or vibration—the following list can always be applied as a substitute for any other leaf you'd like in your recipe. Special attention must be taken when choosing *Ewé Òsíbàtá*, as even though it's the parent leaf for water plants, it should always be accompanied by *Ojúoró* (water lettuce, *Pistia stratiotes*).

By Element of Nature

- Ewé omi (water plants): *Ewé Òsíbàtá* (white water lily: *Nymphaea alha*, family Nymphaeaceae)
- Ewé inón (fire plants): *Ewé Inón* (soapbush: *Clidemia hirta*, family Melastomataceae)
- Ewé afééfé (air plants): *Ewé Afééfé* (nettletree: *Trema micrantha*, family Ulmaceae)
- Ewé ilè or igbó (earth plants): *Ewé Ogbó* (monkey ear: *Periploca nigrescens*, family Apocynaceae)

By Energy

- **Male:** *Ogbó* (monkey ear: *Periploca nigrescens,* family Apocynaceae)
- **Female:** *Gbòrò Ayabá* (bayhops: *Ipomoea pes-caprae*, family Convolvulaceae)

By Vibration

- *Èró* (calm leaves): *Òdúndún* (neverdie: *Kalanchoe crenata*, family Crassulaceae)
- *Gun* (active leaves): *Pèrègún* (corn plant: *Dracaena frangrans*, family Liliaceae)

Rosemary: The Wild-Card Herb

Each leaf, flower, fruit, and seed has specific magical powers and characteristics, and combining them in the right way is the secret to creating a recipe of power. But did you know that rosemary is a type of wild-card herb, one that can be used for many different purposes and can serve as a substitute in most recipes?

Originally from the Mediterranean region, close to the sea cliffs, its name comes from the Romans, who called it *rosmarinus*—"sea dew" in Latin. Rosemary is much appreciated for its aromatic and medicinal virtues; studies have proven that it is capable of combating and preventing numerous health problems, in addition to serving as a powerful aromatizer. It is even said that on its own it is enough to make a complete medicinal and cosmetic pharmacy. Look at some of the therapeutic powers of rosemary:

- Prevents cancer
- Improves memory
- Improves mood
- Combats migraine
- Relieves muscle pain
- Anti-inflammatory
- Strengthens the immune system

- Treats digestive problems
- Helps with hair growth
- Improves circulation
- Helps in respiratory treatments
- Detoxifies the liver
- Anti-aging agent

A many-branched, evergreen shrub with woody stems and small, needle-shaped leaves, rosemary is magically classified as a female plant, belonging to the air element and to the Orisha Oshala, god of all creation. But despite its classification, it is of great help in creating any magic recipe, being considered a wild-card herb. That's right! Because it has so many functions and properties in both natural medicine and magic, rosemary can be used in almost all rituals: for spiritual cleansing, purification, growth, prosperity, happiness, and even love. Choosing rosemary as one of your ingredients is a guarantee of a good choice!

Just to give you an idea, in Egypt, rosemary branches were used in purification rituals, and since ancient times, it has been believed to aid memory. It is no wonder that Greek students had the habit of weaving rosemary branches in their hair when they were studying for exams. It was also used in weddings, burials, churches, and hospitals for good luck and to purify the environment (for antiseptic power). Also, as early as the sixth century, King Charlemagne decreed that rosemary should be planted in all the empire's gardens.

On a psychological level, rosemary strengthens self-esteem, provides courage, and helps children with passive emotional structures who do not respond well to experiencing aggression. It is also excellent for depression, and it works on the notion of physical time, helping with the feeling of being rushed and that we have no time for anything. In medicine, however, rosemary is not recommended for people with high blood pressure, epileptics, alcoholics, and pregnant women, as consuming large amounts of this plant can lead to uterine contractions and miscarriage.

Rosemary is also very easy to plant and grow at home. Just clip a branch and plant it in moist soil, in pots about 20 centimeters in diameter, until it develops roots. When it has grown a little, just transplant the seedling into the garden, where it will grow to almost 1 meter high!

CHAPTER 10

Everything Is Energy

The most fundamental lesson might seem the most obvious, and also the one to which we give the least importance: *we live in a world of energies*. More than that: *we are pure energy, encapsulated in a material body* to enjoy the incarnate life for a short period of time, and during this period, to seek balance, personal evolution, and happiness at every moment. This lesson is beyond magic traditions or holistic-esoteric theories. Even biology and medicine teach it: for the physical body to live, it is necessary that the various organs and systems of the human body, cells, hormones, vitamins, enzymes, molecules, atoms, and subatomic particles combine and transform themselves, absorb the various elements that make up the food and medicines we ingest, and metamorphose the energy obtained from each of them into new energies for the continuity of life on earth.

It might sound like just another cliché phrase from a book on magic, but this is the greatest lesson of all: the way we move our body, the words we say and the tone of voice we use to say them, the everyday actions we take, like opening our eyes in the morning or breathing, the care we take with what we eat and how we care for our body through exercise or therapy, the thoughts that wander through our mind during the day—everything, absolutely everything in us and around us, is made of energy. And when we talk about energies, the rule is clear: *opposites balance, similarities attract*. Rhonda Byrne, author of several bestsellers worldwide and a leading expert on the law of attraction, teaches us that:

Life is simple. It is made of two kinds of things: positive and negative. Each area of your life—be it health, money, relationships, work, or happiness—can have a positive or negative effect. You have too much or too little money. You are healthy or sick. You have happy or complicated relationships. Your career is exciting and successful or boring and unsuccessful. You are always smiling or unhappy. You have pleasant or bad years, good or hard times, happy or sad days. If you identify more negative than positive things in your life, then something is very wrong, and you know it.[28]

Here's the question that cannot stay quiet: are you truly and honestly aware of this? How many and which negative aspects of your life today can you identify the origin, causes, and consequences of without pointing fingers and blaming the environment or the people around you? And on how many of them have you consciously acted to correct and rebalance?

Calm down … I know it's not that easy. If you answered "none" to any of the questions above, relax, as you are definitely no exception: the vast majority of people do. As Deborah L. Price rightly says in the first pages of her book *Terapia da Riqueza* (*Money Therapy*): "We have become so oblivious to the reality of what is actually happening that we are too immobilized to take any action and make the necessary changes to subsist on this planet."[29] So, if we're all stuck together on this sinking ship, it means that despite the problems, *everything is all right*.

I mean … *No, it's not all right!*

---

28. Rhonda Byrne, *O Poder* (Rio de Janeiro: Sextante, 2018). Translated from the Portuguese.

29. Deborah L. Price, *Terapia da Riqueza: 8 Padrões de Comportamento para Criar Prosperidade* (Rio de Janeiro: Best Seller, 2008). Translated from the Portuguese.

It's just ordinary and toxically comfortable to go on like this. After all, any effort to get out of the situation we are living in today might seem more frightening and dangerous than living with the difficulties and blockages that we have become used to facing every day. And do you know what good it will do to read this whole book and practice all possible and imaginable magic rituals if you continue in this way?

Absolutely none!

I'm sorry to tell you that no ritual, no prayer, no magic can transform your life unless you decide to leave behind each one of the chains that bind you in this routine of repeating mistakes and getting used to day-to-day difficulties as if this were the destiny the gods had designed for you. Regardless of religion, each one of us was created in the image and likeness of the gods to ultimately become an individual deity. The sun, the moon, the stars, the wind, the virgin forests, the rain, the rivers and waterfalls, the air we breathe, the roads we walk on, and each of the living beings we cross paths with in our daily lives is a divine spark to which we can connect, combining and multiplying vibrations and victories. When we learn once and for all that *we are pure energy, encapsulated in a material body,* we will also learn that we can manipulate that same energy to combine and transform it according to our best wishes.

When we begin to act objectively on each of the aspects that make up our life, we also begin to take responsibility, make choices, and determine the results we get in our daily lives. This does not mean that our lives will be free of unforeseen circumstances or challenges that we'll have to deal with and overcome. However, this does mean that through small changes in our routine, we can achieve great things—greater than we can imagine.

When we understand that everything is energy and, being energy, that everything can be balanced and activated in our favor, we will then take care of the environment in which we live and work, prepare the food we eat, and choose the people we live with and the words we say in a magical way—and this is, after all, the big secret!

CHAPTER 11

Consciousness & Purpose

By understanding and accepting that everything in the Universe is pure energy—including ourselves—and that every action we take and every result we get in our lives is a reflection of the choices we make or don't make, we also come to understand that we are uniquely responsible for each and every one of these results. After all, if everything is a combination and transformation of the various energies around us, when we choose to change them, we also choose to change the result we will arrive at. In the same way, when we choose not to act and simply let things take their course (which, in other words, means letting outside factors alter and influence the energies around us and within us), we are nevertheless making a decision for which we must take responsibility. By assuming we are the only ones responsible for what happens to us, we become aware that every attitude, every action, no matter how big or small, every word, every feeling, and every event around us is the result of what we do or fail to do.

At this moment, several questions must be running through your mind, questioning what I am saying. You may be wondering, "So am I responsible for someone who hurts me?" or "How can I be responsible for going out and having an accident?" or something like that, right? To this, I can answer you simply and directly: of course, even when we become aware that everything is energy and that we can change it at will, we will always be subject to random events that can surprise us on a daily basis—after all, none of us can control which or how external factors affect us. But even so, no matter how severe a challenge we face may be, we can always control how much it emotionally affects us, how we act in and react to the situation, and what the vibration and the energy is that we emanate when managing the events around us. So, in the end, even if we cannot take responsibility for what happens to us, we *can* take responsibility for the way we deal with it!

Can you see the difference?

Taking responsibility for what happens to us is called *becoming aware* or *becoming conscious*. The Michaelis Dictionary defines *consciousness* as:

1. The capacity, of an intellectual and emotional nature, that a human being has to consider or recognize external (object, quality, situation) or interior reality, such as, for example, the modifications of his own self;

2. The sense or perception that allows a person to know moral values or commandments, as to right or wrong, and apply them in different situations, approving or disapproving of his own actions, so that he establishes inner judgments that provide him with feelings of joy, peace, satisfaction, etc., and from which result convictions as to honor, righteousness, responsibility, or duty fulfilled, or, in contrast, remorse or guilt;

3. The set of ideas, beliefs, and attitudes of a group of people concerning the surrounding world or everything they have in common; knowledge, conviction, and understanding;

4. The human being himself understood as a thinking being or spiritual entity; soul, spirit, mind.[30]

Now, think with me: if we are responsible for everything that happens around us or, ultimately, we are responsible for the way we deal with the challenges and difficulties that come our way … can we also manipulate, manage, and be responsible for the good things that happen to us? The answer to that is also very simple: *Yes!*

The Universe makes no distinction between right and wrong, good and evil, positive and negative: all of these exist here, now, and at the same time. The Universe is, in short, an inexhaustible source of energy at our disposal—and becoming conscious of it is the first step toward achieving your goals. However, I repeat: you must always keep in mind that, when it comes to energy, the rule is clear: *opposites balance, similarities attract.* Search your memory and answer honestly: how many times, on a bad day when everything seemed to go wrong, was your instinctive reaction to complain and keep on vibrating negatively? Now tell me: in how many of those situations did the result become different from receiving even more negativity? And how many other problems and bad situations kept happening soon after, making you ask yourself, "Is there no end to this?"

Based on the process of consciousness we are talking about, it is easy to see how it is possible to change what happens to us in two simple ways: *balance* and *attraction*. To do this, when we are faced with adverse situations or negative feelings, *we can vibrate and offer the opposite—the positive—to balance the energy we do not want.* Similarly, when we encounter positive situations or feelings

---

30. *Dicionário Brasileiro da Língua Portuguesa*, Michaelis Online, accessed September 28, 2019, http://michaelis.uol.com.br. Translated from the Portuguese.

in our day-to-day lives, *we can vibrate and offer the similar—again the positive—to attract even more of what is good for us.*

The most impressive thing about this formula is that, once applied and extended to every small or big event in our everyday life, it expands and multiplies. By vibrating positively about a specific negative situation, you balance it out and, with this, also nullify (in whole or in part) its effect. At the same time, by vibrating positively, you also begin to demonstrate what you want to attract—more positivity. Since the law says that "like attracts like," by offering positivity, what will you receive in return? New positivities!

This almost mathematical dynamic recalls the concept of "the gift" established by French sociologist and anthropologist Marcel Mauss (1872–1950). In his book *The Gift*, Mauss talks about the forms of exchange in primitive societies, and his work is recognized as an important study on reciprocity and the exchange of things between people. In a simplified way, Mauss's research states that all human relationships, physical or symbolic, are based on gift dynamics: give, receive, and reciprocate. In the article "The Sociology of Marcel Mauss: The Gift, Symbolism, and Association" (published in Portuguese in *Revista Crítica de Ciências Sociais*), which discusses the social and political implications of Mauss's theory, the author tells us that:

> The gift is present everywhere and does not only concern isolated and discontinuous moments of reality. What circulates has various names: it is called money, cars, furniture, clothes, but also smiles, kindnesses, words, hospitality, gifts, free services, among many others. ... Unlike other animals, the human is characterized by the presence of the will, the pressure of conscience from

one onto others, the communication of ideas, language, aesthetic arts, by groupings and religions, in a word, he adds, the "institutions that are the feature of our life in common."[31]

Although Mauss's theory deals with practical issues in the relationships within human societies, from his concept of "the gift" it is possible to understand the dynamics of the energies of which we speak: if I *give* negatively, I also *receive* negatively and *reciprocate* in the same way; whereas if I *give* positively, I *receive* positively and, therefore, *reciprocate* positively. Since all of this has already been happening automatically, imagine the fantastic results we could achieve by *consciously* using this same dynamic!

In African spiritual traditions, this practice is taken even further: those who believe in the strength and power of the Orishas experience the gift almost daily, even when they are not aware of it. When we make our offerings of thanks for the blessings received, when we light a candle to strengthen our requests' intentions, when we praise the Orishas through songs and ritual dances: every act dedicated to the Orishas is a gift that, due to the spiritual character of religious practice, gains two new components: *magic* and *purpose*. Back to word analysis, the Michaelis Dictionary defines *magic* as "the practice based on the belief that it is possible, through the intervention of supernatural and fantastic beings, to produce inexplicable, special, irrational and supernatural effects, through formulas and rituals." The same Michaelis Dictionary also defines the meaning of *purpose* as "the intention

31. Paulo Henrique Martins, "A Sociologia de Marcel Mauss: Dádiva, Simbolismo e Associação," *Revista Crítica de Ciências Sociais* 73 (2005): 45–66, https://journals.openedition.org/rccs/954#tocto1n2. Translated from the Portuguese.

to do or not do something; design, plan, project, will. Decision after consideration of several possibilities; deliberation."[32]

In this way, we can affirm that any act of devotion or ritual performed to the Orishas is, in itself, an act of magic. After all, we believe that the Orishas' strength and power are capable of producing inexplicable effects in our lives. At the same time, an act of magic is always guided by the motivation to achieve a goal. Whoever makes a request, asks for something; whoever gives thanks, expresses gratitude for some result. Therefore, the practice of spirituality is based precisely on the union of these three aspects: *consciousness*—I know what I'm doing and I do it by my own free will; *magic*—I seek divine intervention to transform the energies of the ritual elements into supernatural results; and *purpose*—I have a specific goal for what I'm doing.

To move forward, however, we need to remember a fundamental factor: none of these three aspects exempts us from taking *responsibility* for what we are seeking, for what we are doing from now until we achieve the desired result, and, especially, for what we will do after we fulfill our desires or achieve our purpose. "Give, receive, and reciprocate" is a cyclical and continuous process. It grows and expands as we practice it, and therefore, this cycle should not be broken by those who genuinely seek to live in harmony, happiness, and prosperity, no longer merely in the image and likeness of the gods, but in fact, becoming a living deity themselves.

---

32. Michaelis Online.

CHAPTER 12

Three Bodies, One Life

When we combine consciousness, magic, purpose, and responsibility, our life starts to harmonize with the energies around us. Yet not everything is as simple as it seems: every change begins within us, and it is with these changes that we can truly act. For this idea of change to become real, we need to understand of what and how we are made, so that we can align each internal aspect with the external aspects that are similar to the vibrations we seek.

As reflections of the gods, human beings are basically made up of three bodies that overlap and complement each other on an energetic level: (1) the physical body, (2) the mental body, and (3) the spiritual body. These three bodies exist at the same time and are indispensable to each other so that each one of us can perform our functions and pursue our goals during our life on earth. No human being can have one of these three bodies without, necessarily, having the others. Still, to live in a healthy and balanced way, the three bodies need to be cared for equally and be balanced and harmonized.

Physical Body

The first body is the *physical body*—the matter in which we are imprisoned during our incarnate life—with which medicine and biology are concerned. Formed by its various organs and tissues, simple and complex systems of cells with diverse functions, the physical body is the receptacle of the two other bodies that we will see below, and precisely for this reason, taking care of it is of utmost importance.

Like the mental and spiritual bodies, the physical body is constantly changing and growing. It is the only one of the three that we can actually see and watch the development of: the union of an egg and a sperm fertilizes a fetus that, gradually and according to the care received, will grow and develop until it becomes a human body out in the world. According to this care and through proper nutrition and physical exercise, this body's shape and size can be changed. In the same way, lack of care and mistreatment of the physical body can make us weak and sick—everything, again, is a matter of choice and responsibility.

All this care is based on what we ingest—whether it's food, drink, or a remedy, which will be processed by the organs of the various systems and then transformed into energy. Who among us hasn't heard that a glass of wine a day prevents cancer or hasn't learned that it is necessary to eat foods that contain fiber to keep the digestive system functioning well? Who hasn't heard about foods that promote weight loss or improve cholesterol levels? However, no one considers that in addition to choosing the right food and drink for a balanced *physical* diet, these same choices can be transformed at the energetic level so that, in addition to their biological function, they can also perform *magical* functions.

Mental Body

The second body is the *mental body*, the subjective universe formed by the set of experiences and cultural and social influences encountered throughout our entire existence, which forms and determines our personality and how we think, act, and react to the external world. If the physical body is the building that houses us during our life on earth, the mental body is the foundation that supports that building. From this analogy, we can understand the importance of taking care of the mental body so that the other two bodies, physical and spiritual, can coexist in a harmonious and healthy way.

Our mental body is formed by all our thoughts, feelings, emotions, and perceptions of the world. These change as we age and experience different situations in life, whether good or bad, creating a complex network of interpretations and individual combinations capable of molding and adapting us to the environment in which we live. Our personality is formed precisely through the development of and interrelationship between these aspects of the mental body and the outside world, as well as the social and cultural factors to which we are exposed from birth—how we show ourselves to the world and how we are perceived by it.

Interested in its significance, many scholars worldwide have devoted their time and research to discovering the mysteries of the human mind and finding ways to develop its potential. The work of Sigmund Freud, who is considered the father of modern psychoanalysis, was the precursor to these studies. In 1923 he presented a theory that divided the human mind into three interdependent parts: *id*, *ego*, and *superego*.

According to Freud's theory, the id is the most primary power of the human being, the animal instinct that dwells within each of us. Irrational, the id is formed by the impulses—instincts, organic urges, and unconscious desires working according to the "pleasure principle"; that is, it seeks to realize and experience pleasure while avoiding everything painful or unpleasant, regardless of any social or moral limitations that may exist and that would suppress the possibility of realizing these desires. For all this, the id ignores judgment, logic, values, ethics, and morals. It is demanding, impulsive, blind, irrational, antisocial, and selfish.

The ego, in turn, is the part of the human mind governed by the "reality principle," responsible for rational reasoning, and it develops from the id as the baby becomes aware of the world around it and is introduced to reason, planning, and waiting for the moment when reality will allow the satisfaction of its impulses. The ego mediates between the id's instinctive principles and the superego's idealized principles, preventing our mind's unconscious contents from taking the place of its conscious contents, triggering defense mechanisms against this.

The superego is the moral part of the human psyche, representing society's values, the ideal and virtually unattainable state, the perfection that considers and equalizes the wills of all beings. It is divided into two subsystems: the *ego ideal*, which represents the good to be sought, attained, and achieved, and the *moral conscience*, which determines the evil to be avoided. With this, the superego has three main functions: to inhibit impulses contrary to the idealized rules dictated by itself; to force the ego to comply with these rules; and to lead the individual to perfection by suppressing the impulses of the id.

Just as the physical body is subject to illness, the mental body is subject to various psychological illnesses precisely because of the dynamics and balances among these three parts of the mental body. A psychopath, for example, has an overly dominant id and a significantly diminished superego, which strips them of remorse and empathy, highlighting their lack of moral conscience. In the same way, depression and mania—two sides of the same coin—are also considered psychological illnesses with their origin in the imbalance among these aspects of the mental body.

On the other hand, just as the physical body can be cared for and shaped through the choice of food and exercise, or even through the remedies of traditional medicine, the mental body can also be shaped and modified through the various modalities of therapeutic and psychoanalytic sessions, through the practice of meditation and exercises such as mindfulness, or even through techniques to improve what is known as neuroplasticity, researched and applied by neuroscience theories. All these alternatives can also be enhanced through the use of magical rituals that balance and harmonize our mental frequencies. They alter our levels of consciousness and activate sensitive fields of the psyche, such as a smell memory that reminds us of and brings us feelings of well-being.

Spiritual Body

The third body is the *spiritual body*, the divine portion that lives within each of us and that expands through the other two bodies beyond the limitations of time, space, and matter. Regardless of the name or number of the gods and goddesses we believe in, the spiritual body reflects these deities, through which we connect to the sacred egregores and become the continuation and continuity of life. In the book *A Arte do Benzimento* (*The Art of Blessing*), author Javert de Menezes cites a survey conducted by Dr. Harold G. Koening of Duke University, which says:

> An exhaustive analysis of more than 1,500 reputable medical studies indicates that people who are more religious and pray more have better mental and physical health. Of 125 studies that looked at the relationship between health and worship, 85 showed that regular believers live longer.[33]

---

33. Javert Menezes, *A Arte do Benzimento: Orações, Rezas, Benzeduras* (São Paulo: Editora Alfabeto, 2017).

The author further states, about the results of this research, that:

> The benefits of religious practice have shown that people live better, in general concerning stress, when they have particular involvement with a faith community or a religious commitment. Generally, these people experience greater well-being because they have more confidence, become more optimistic, develop less depression, less anxiety, and commit less suicide. They also have stronger immune systems, lower blood pressure, and probably better cardiovascular function.[34]

Like physical and mental bodies, the spiritual body is also constantly evolving and developing. Some traditions, especially more spiritualist ones such as Kardecism and Umbanda, believe in the evolution of the spirit as a way of purification in the presence of the carnal practices and vices of the physical body, seeking the "enlightenment" that will be enjoyed mainly after disincarnation from matter. Other traditions, such as Candomblé, believe in the evolution of the spirit in a more direct and objective sense. In these traditions, we strengthen our relationship and connection with the Orishas in the here and now through magical rituals and ethical and moral improvement, through the daily practice of good deeds, seeking to enhance our personal and collective experience during incarnate life through the divine influence on our destinies.

Therefore, *Ori* plays a fundamental role in this evolution. "The head"—both physical and symbolic, from which all Candomblé rituals are performed—has absolute importance in the process of spiritual growth from the point of view of this tra-

---

34. Ibid.

dition, because it is considered the connection point among the three bodies—physical, mental, and spiritual. At the same time, Ori is also considered an Orisha, thought of as an individual deity that makes each human being unique and that, like all other deities, must be praised and made offerings to through specific rituals. A popular Yoruba saying goes, *"Ori buruku kosi Orisà,"* which means, "A bad head has no Orisha!"

If the physical body is the building and the mental body is the foundation that supports the structure that constitutes our life on earth, then the spiritual body is the ground where these foundations are laid and established. In the same way, just as the physical and mental bodies can be affected by diseases, the spiritual body is also subject to attacks and imbalances that, in my opinion, are more serious, because they reflect from it onto the other two bodies and harm life as a whole—after all, as the famous saying goes, a castle is not built on sand. Consequently, just as important as seeking treatments and medicine to cure the illnesses of the body and mind, when the spiritual body suffers it is urgent and fundamental to seek spiritual remedies to heal it—the so-called *ebós*, the magical rituals of the Orishas that aim to rebalance and strengthen the spirit, canceling the effects of what makes us suffer.

The Invisible Glue That Binds the Three Bodies

As we learned at the beginning of this book, in African spirituality every malaise or illness at the physical or mental level occurs first at the spiritual level, making it necessary to seek healing through magic rituals (which will take care of the causes) and the treatments of conventional medicine, psychology, and psychiatry (which will take care of the consequences). However, there is a fundamental factor that acts, precisely, as the "glue" that binds and interrelates these bodies, allowing the growth of one to help and favor the development and evolution of the other, and, in the case of illnesses, one also ends up affecting the other. We call this "glue" *energy*.

With a complicated definition beyond physical and mathematical concepts, energy is the force that allows the different systems and bodies to carry out actions and transformations within themselves and around them. Invisible, energy is the fulfilling potential in everything and everyone, even when we are not aware of it or do not awaken it. Although it is related to the spiritual aspects—after all, where there is spirit, there is energy—energy has nothing to do with religion: according to the law of the conservation of mass, also known as Lavoisier's principle, named after French scientist Antoine Lavoisier, energy and matter cannot appear out of nowhere and cannot be destroyed; the only possibility is to modify it—hence the famous phrase "In nature, nothing is created, nothing is lost, everything is transformed," which represents very well the general principles of what we call *magic*.

When we talk about magic, energy is the invisible force that can come from nature or from deities and that can be accessed and manipulated in order to transform the reality around us according to our goals. Every object, every item of food, every element of nature, every living being, and every leaf, flower, seed, or root has distinct energies. Similarly, each magical tradition around the world recognizes a different potential in each of these energies and, in their traditions, establishes specific rules and rites so that they can be combined and, together, interfere from the spiritual plane (through the influence of the deities) and mental plane (through the establishment of a purpose or objective) in our physical reality (through the fulfillment of goals).

With that, we can see that energy is really the "glue" that binds the physical, mental, and spiritual bodies together and that this same energy is in everything and everyone around us, including ourselves. By learning the secrets of how to access and manipulate it in the right way, we can then practice magic all the time and transform even everyday acts into magical acts. An example of this comes in Candomblé, Umbanda, and all other religions and traditions of African origin: in them, magic is a daily reality, and it can be accessed and performed both in very complicated ways—such as in the offerings to the Orishas, which may contain various foods and, in some cases, even animal sacrifices, which can only be performed by priests and priestesses prepared for these acts—and in simple and ordinary ways—such as in baths and fumigations using the power of sacred plants, which can be performed by anyone who studies their teachings and execution techniques.

In the herbal witchcraft of the Orishas, each leaf, each flower, and each seed or fruit carries within itself a particular universe of powers and energies available to those who, with *responsibility, consciousness,* and *purpose,* decide to access them and use them in their rituals. Knowing these powers and understanding the dynamics with which the energies pass between the various bodies, combine, and transform themselves is the key to making the magic come true. The first step in this is to understand that everything we can see is only a reflection of what has been previously established in the mental and spiritual planes.

CHAPTER 13

Self-Care & Personal Protection

When we think of magic, what immediately comes to mind is performing rituals to solve all the problems around us and conquer whatever our goals are, like a magic trick, right? But ... how many times have you seen things work out just like that? As we have already seen, performing magic rituals is only one part of a complex whole that works almost mathematically: the different physical-mental-spiritual bodies, in the different traditions and religions all over the world, combine and influence each other on an energetic level. In turn, this energy neutralizes or attracts other energies similar to it through the dynamics of the gift (give-receive-reciprocate) and can—according to specific rules and magic fundamentals—be manipulated in order to, only then, materialize what we want with consciousness, responsibility, and purpose.

Complex ... indeed, it is very complex! So the first step in transforming your life and the simplest acts in your daily life into true magic rituals is to understand that there is a logical sequence of care that needs to be followed. We often look at the specific goal we are seeking but then forget to recognize the universal context into which this problem or desire is placed: as we've seen, rituals of prosperity, for example, do not always mean attracting money but rather avoiding scarcity. Similarly, rituals of love may not be directly related to bringing someone to you and making them like you; these cases often have more to do with warding off loneliness and cultivating self-love—love from outside comes automatically, through the gift. Do you see how mathematical these dynamics look?

Having understood that, the second step is to go back a few pages and see that many of them were dedicated to dealing with the most important and fundamental focus of care that we should have in the practice of magic: our body—or rather, our bodies. *Yes, all of them*: physical, mental, and spiritual. For each of them, one medicine, one magic; after all, *our body is our temple!* We live so accustomed to the harassment caused by the frenetic pace of the modern world that, most of the time, we believe that our body is a tireless and infallible machine, at the disposal of all our *anxieties and busy schedules and work commitments and parties with friends*, which leads us to being *short on time* and leads us to being *short of breath* until our body *lacks the willingness to wake up* and …

Hey, breathe! Breathe, and don't freak out! Breathe and repeat: Our body is our temple! Our body is our temple! Take a deep breath and repeat it again … Now, slowly, notice how everything seems to become lighter, even if only a little. See? Our bodies are not tireless and infallible machines. They are delicate machines, willing to take us much further than we can imagine today, but they need to be cared for to take us there.

When we truly understand that these are plural bodies, and that matter, mind, and spirit combine, collaborate, and influence each other, we begin to understand what self-care means. It's not just going on a diet or going to the gym; it's not just going to therapy or practicing meditation; it's not just going to a religious temple and practicing spirituality and faith. It's all this mixed together—and for each of them, one medicine, one magic.

Whenever we plan a magic ritual, regardless of the objective we wish to achieve, we must first ask ourselves: *are our bodies protected and prepared for it?* Magic is the manipulation of energy forces; it's the gift in action; it's directing a specific energy to undo another and attract a third. Based on this dynamic, in every ritual there is an exchange process and the movement of forces from one side to the other—and for negative energy to be removed, our bodies need to be prepared to face it and be protected not to absorb it. That's why, very often, the same magical ritual works excellently for one person and does not work at all for another. The same herbs, the same moon phase, the same prayers and invocations, everything the same—except for the result. Why did it change then? It changed because the bodies weren't the same and, indeed, because one of them was more prepared than the other.

Thinking this way, you can't hope to practice magic while living like a shoemaker whose son always goes barefoot. The first and most important ritual to be performed is that in which we take care of our own selves, strengthening ourselves in matter, mind, and spirit in a constant way. Only then will we be prepared to access and manipulate the outer energies and shape reality in our favor. But, how to take care of and protect ourselves? Here are some simple and handy tips. (Also, whenever you are going to perform a ritual, it is vital to observe your vibration and energy at that specific moment and, if you do not feel in harmony, at least take a fresh herbal bath before beginning it.)

Physical Body

What to do?

- Go to sleep and wake up early.
- Rest at least eight hours a day.
- Eat balanced meals.
- Consume juices and natural foods.
- Drink at least two liters of water per day.
- Practice sports or exercise.

- Take care of personal hygiene.
- Have an active sex life.

What not to do?

- Consume fat and sugar.
- Smoke cigarettes.
- Drink excessive alcoholic beverages.
- Take drugs.
- Have unprotected sex.
- Self-medicate.
- Expose yourself to rain or moisture, especially on the back and feet.
- Make excessive physical effort.

Mental Body

What to do?

- Practice meditation or mindfulness.
- Breathe consciously.
- Choose the words you speak, communicating without violence or aggression.
- Regularly and daily give thanks.
- Visit friends and laugh often.
- Truly see the people around you, practicing empathy.
- Choose your news sources; after all, you don't need to expose yourself to random negativity on TV or the internet.
- Recognize your mistakes and flaws, but value your strengths and good qualities above them.

What not to do?

- Curse or say aggressive words.
- Anticipate suffering and problems and feed anxiety.
- Internalize pain and distress.
- Swallow your tears and hold a grudge.
- Live in a state of tension and fear.
- Maintain toxic or disempowering relationships.
- Watch violent movies and TV series, especially before bedtime.
- Demand perfection from yourself and others—after all, everyone makes mistakes.

Spiritual Body

What to do?

- Pray and express gratitude daily.
- Take weekly herbal baths.
- Fumigate your house and work spaces.
- Attend a Candomblé terreiro or any other religious temple.
- Get to know your Birth Odus [35] and enhance their positive aspects.
- Consult the cowrie-shell divination at least once a year and perform the indicated rituals.
- Practice the principles of the gift, trusting in the Sacred—the secret is to *believe*.

---

35. Want to discover your Birth Odu? Access www.diegodeoxossi .com.br/my-birth-odu and sign up for free!

What not to do?

- Make promises and not keep them.
- Perform magic rituals without knowledge.
- Disrespect your priest or magical initiator.
- Visit hospitals, funerals, or cemeteries when not necessary.
- Try to establish relationships of exchange or bargaining with deities.
- Violate the taboos of your Birth Odu or your ruling Orisha.
- Fail to apply the restrictions and precautions before and after magical rituals.
- Mix esoteric or religious traditions and practices—each has its own foundations.

CHAPTER 14

Healing Blessings & Prayers: The Power of Words

In all commonly known religions, we can find the practice of using spoken words as a plea to the deities to intercede on behalf of someone's physical well-being. Especially in Brazil, due to the mixing of the different races that formed our people, pure and simple prayer practices were mixed with indigenous knowledge about the use of herbs, which, in addition to their energetic aspects, were also used for their medicinal aspects. In the same way, the syncretism between the Catholic saints and the African Orishas, carried by enslaved Blacks in the holds of slave ships, added to these practices the ancestral wisdom of magic, giving rise to the tradition of the "healer women." Who among us has never seen or heard of an old woman who, with a sprig of rue or rosemary in her hand, would bless the bodies of children to cure them of illnesses such as shingles and "stuck rib" or to remove the evil eye?

These ladies, wise guardians of popular spiritual culture, were and still are true libraries of wisdom and prayers for any illnesses of the body, mind, or spirit. Empirically, they know the powers of each herb and each leaf, and above all, they know as well as anyone else how to resignify them and intuitively replace them when they cannot find the specific species they were looking for. Unfortunately, the tradition of these healer women has been lost over the years, and nowadays, it is no longer common to find them in big cities. However, the cultural and religious exchange between indigenous, African, and popular practices has left us a series of lessons that we can apply to our daily rituals, and if we no longer have access to the ancient prayers used by the wise old ladies, we learned from them that pronouncing sacred words with faith and devotion can awaken the power of the leaves so that, according to what we ask for in words, we can bring about the transformation in matter. From all this, the most valuable lesson is, really, to understand that *words have power* and that the same kind of leaf can be used for different purposes, precisely because, when singing to enchant, we awaken a specific aspect of its magical potential.

Moreover, it is also important to go back to the concept of magical balance and inequality learned in the previous chapters: in general terms, the goal of healing blessings is to heal physical or spiritual ills, remove the negative energies that materialized the problem, and then make the physical body return to its original state of health. In this way, herbal healing blessings should always be performed in an odd number: one, three, five, or seven different species, balanced and harmonized according to the healing being sought.

The steps for performing the rituals for healing blessings are quite simple, and their effects are enhanced when the chosen herbs and words of power are combined with consciousness and purpose. Basically, they consist of five steps:

1. In a quiet place without outside interference, position the person, animal, or object to be blessed facing the person who will perform the healing blessing.

2. Both of them take three deep breaths to focus their consciousness on the present moment, and the giver of the healing blessing asks the person being blessed, also three times, if he or she truly wants to receive the ritual and then listens to the answer. This step

is vital in creating a connection between the two of them and the deities that will be invoked.

3. The healer then makes the prayers to and invokes the deities who will work with him in the spiritual plane in order to cure the ailments he proposes to cure.

4. Once this is done, with light movements, the healer rubs the chosen leaves and herbs over the body of the person being blessed while reciting the chosen words of power; the prayer should be repeated at least three times, until the number of herbal species selected for the ritual is reached.

5. After praying, the leaves and herbs must be immediately thrown out on the street or back into nature. Only after the leaves have been dispatched will the person who received the healing blessing be released from the ritual and be able to go about his or her normal routine.

Some traditional recipes for healing blessings also include other elements such as water, charcoal, ashes, and so on. In the chapters to follow, we will learn a little more about elements and ingredients that can be added to our rituals and their meanings, so it is important to pay attention to your intuition when planning your rituals because it will show you whether and which of them should be used.

Another critical aspect is to remember that magic is made up of symbolism. Therefore, the gestures performed are often essential during the rituals, and they must always be in accordance with what you are asking and praying for. Some very common examples are:

Chapter 14

- If you are blessing a skin problem like shingles or a rash, when praying for the disease to leave the body being blessed, you can touch the wounds lightly with the branch of the herbs being used and shake it forcefully in the air as if you were literally "shaking off" and throwing away what you touched.

- If during the ritual your words of power dictate to "go away" or something like that, you can touch the body of the person being blessed with the branch of herbs and ask him to blow on the branch hard, symbolizing that departure.

- At the end of a ritual that aims to break negative forces, pronounce the word "break" or "I break you" at the very moment you break the branch of herbs with your hands and throw it away.

Another aspect that can be added to your healing blessings is the laying on of hands to direct energies to the person being blessed, as a kind of a spiritual transfer, a common practice in Umbanda and Reiki. In this case, always remember that *responsibility* is the key word. Therefore, this kind of magical act should only be done by those who already have experience in this type of ritual. In addition, it is always important to close your ritual by thanking the invoked deities and also the person being blessed, creating a bond of trust and affection between you.

CHAPTER 15

Our House, Our Temple

Like our body, our house is also our temple. After all, it is where we keep our intimacies, receive our loved ones, strengthen our dreams, and build our plans. Even so, it is very common for us not to treat our home or our work environment the right way, assuming that it is *just the place where we work and live.* However, when we realize how the energies of everything and everyone around us influence us and combine to form new energies, neutralizing opposite energies and attracting like energies, we also begin to realize that the environments around us affect and influence us, and vice versa. In this way, if we can't control the energies that are in the outside world, we can at least favor and balance those where we spend most of our lives.

Most of the time, however, it is common to imagine that taking care of the house's energies is just a matter of eventually doing an energy cleansing with ammonia and fumigating, or with the Blue Ritual, whose recipe is given at the end of this book. Of course, these "heavy" cleanings are important, especially when we feel that the energies around us are more "charged" than usual. Nevertheless—and precisely because these are strong rituals indicated only for specific situations— more important than doing them occasionally is taking care of these energies daily; remember the famous saying: "An ounce of prevention is worth a pound of cure." In addition, it is also important to realize that each room in our house has different and well-defined functions and energies, which must be cared for and harmonized in different ways, like one big ecosystem in harmony.

Creating Power Pots

A very effective way to keep each room's energies aligned with its function is through potted plants or jars of grain specifically created for each of our purposes. To do this, it's quite simple:

1. Using the principles of magical balance and inequality, choose the plants that will be part of our *power pot*.

2. Choose a pot or container that fits the required size and prepare the soil and fertilizers to be used.

3. To activate the energetic function of your power pot and awaken the specific power of each chosen herb, as you put the soil in the pot and plant each species, recite the specific incantation for each of them.

4. At the same time, so that your power pot's energy will be maintained over time, it is also important to plant your incantations. To do so, with a new pencil and on a piece of blank white paper, write the same incantations that you will pronounce and place them next to the roots.

5. When you have finished assembling your power pot, put it in the place where it should do its magical work, always remembering to water it at the right time and with the right amount of water needed for the chosen species.

- **Important**: Just as each room of the house has specific functions and energies that must be taken care of, each power pot will also have them, and you may want to create more than one power pot for the same room: one for protection, another for attraction. For example, remember to observe the moon phase and the ideal day of the week in which to create them.

Protecting Our House

Entrance Gate

The entrance gate is the main point of the house to be protected, being kept well lit and with nothing obstructing the view of the passageway. It is also the most susceptible to strange energies; after all, it is through it that all the people who enter the house pass and also where strangers on the street pass by. In the more traditional Candomblé temples, for example, the house's external wall and its main gate are usually protected by peregum seedlings.

Therefore, it is important to protect the entrance gate with a large pot of male/hot leaves, belonging to the fire element, preferably under the regency of Eshu and Ogun, such as various chili peppers, snake plant, or gale-of-the-wind, along with three iron spears facing upward, like a triple lightning rod. This pot can be made in any phase of the moon, on a Monday or Tuesday, and should be positioned to the left of those entering the residence. To balance its vibrations and attract good energies into the house, to the right side of the entrance gate you can also place a pot of the same size with male and female plants of the elements of earth and water, in order to attract happiness, harmony, and prosperity, ruled by any of the female Orishas or by Oshossi, Shango, or Logunede.

The Front Yard

Just like the main gate, the front yard of the house is also a point that needs attention, as it is through it that you will direct the energies you wish to attract into the house. Moreover, it is also in the front yard that you can place power pots to nullify negative energies and vibrations that may pass through the gate. Want an example? Looking into the backyard from the main gate, identify the first and nearest point where your eyes reach— it's right there that you'll position a power pot with dumb cane and seven small mirrors facing the street to ward off incoming envy and the evil eye. Like the pot for defending the gate, this can also be made during any moon phase, and preferably on a Monday or Tuesday.

After the main pot—and especially if the distance from the gate to the house is long— you can plant a sequence of seven species of flowers or aromatic herbs that attract good company, harmony, and happiness, ruled mainly by the earth and fire elements—such as those of Oshossi, Logunede, Oshun, and Iansã. Plant the chosen species from the strongest to the softest, creating a corridor that invites you to enter the house. Just as the energies from the street can be harmful, our happiness also comes from there, and this "trail" invites the good energies to enter our home.

Main Living Room

The main living room is where we will receive visitors and socialize with our loved ones. Besides being one of the places in the house where we should take care of cleaning and decoration the most, it is also important that people feel at ease and comfortable while in it. Therefore, scattering small power pots or grain jars that activate good communication and exchange of experiences, with air and water plants decorated with coins, is an excellent option. Another important aspect is to define the position in which the main armchair of the owner of the house will be placed and put next to it a power pot with leaves ruled by the earth element that will stimulate confidence, wisdom, and leadership.

The living room is also the place where we gather our family and relax when we are home. Therefore, in addition to the pots that enhance communication and well-being, it is also important to create power pots that favor mental and emotional rest, affection, and harmony, with species ruled by the element of air or even with wind chimes in the living room windows. In either case, the pots should be created preferably during a waxing or new moon, on Wednesdays or Saturdays.

If it is not possible to prepare the power pots for the main entrance gate because your house has no front yard or because you live in an apartment, you can instead create miniature versions of the pots described above and place them immediately behind the front door of the main living room.

Dining Room

Just like the living room, the dining room is also a place for socializing, and the same guidelines apply to it. However, it is important to balance them with colder leaves to promote digestion and well-being. Floral table arrangements with warm colors, such as red and orange, work well; however, avoid using herbs or plants that give off too much perfume, as this can affect the taste of food and disharmonize the moments you'll have there. Another option is to install a fireplace in the living or dining room, where in addition to activating the energy of the fire element, you will also be able to burn dried herbs for fumigations.

Kitchen and Pantry

The kitchen and the pantry are the rooms of the house in which we can most easily activate the magic of power pots. That's where we store and prepare food, so every meal can turn into a ritual. Also, if you store your grains, spices, and pantry supplies in jars instead of in their original packaging, you can use these same jars as containers for your rituals—just enchant them when it comes to storing and, if you like, place inside each of them your incantation written on a fresh sheet of white paper. A tip: On a Thursday during a waxing or full moon, prepare a power pot by mixing a handful of each grain, seed, and other foodstuff you have in your home, offering it to Oshossi and determining in your incantations that food will always be plentiful and abundant in your home.

The stove is always a point of attention in the kitchen's energetic balance: the more burners, the better! At the same time, it is important to position power pots with plants ruled by the elements of earth and water next to it, to balance its strength. An alternative is to create a small magic garden in your kitchen, which, besides magic, will also serve as a source of fresh spices and condiments to use in your culinary recipes.

Master Bedroom

Much more than just a place where we put our bed, a bedroom is a sacred place within our home: it is in it, after all, that we rest, dream, love, and meditate even without meaning to. Therefore, taking care of the energies of the couple's or homeowner's bedroom is of utmost importance, so that it becomes an environment that is both relaxing and able to provide moments of pleasure, where couples feel welcomed and protected, but also desired and sensual.

In addition to the power pots that harmonize the cohabitation of the couple, that favor relaxation and mental and physical rest, and that enhance the libido and the love between the couple, other magical aspects should also be considered when planning the ideal bedroom. The main one is the bed and its position in the room. Regarding this, *feng shui*—an ancient Chinese tradition that acts on the harmonization of the energies in physical spaces through the manipulation and positioning of objects, colors, and decorative items, correcting possible misalignments through these elements—teaches us that:

> The bed should always be facing the entrance door of the room, preferably in the corner opposite the door.... If it is not possible to place the bed in the corner opposite the entrance [of the room], place a mirror in a position that allows those lying down to see the entrance door.... However, care must be taken not to place the bed with the feet facing the door, so that the vital energy of those lying on it will not be lost.... If this is not possible ... this problem can be corrected with a crystal ball or wind chime between the bed and the door.... A room where the head of the bed is toward a door or window is also not considered favorable. One should place a folding screen or other object that opposes the flow of energy that crosses through the entrance and steals the energy of those who sleep.[36]

Besides the suggestions indicated by feng shui, power pots can also be used as an alternative to balance and (re)direct these energies in the master bedroom. In addition, you can also use the same technique as the pots to create small *magic pillows*,

---

36. Celso Yamamoto, *Feng Shui: A Arquitetura Sagrada do Oriente*, 2nd ed. (São Paulo: Ground, 1997).

which will be placed inside the usual pillows or under the mattress or bed furniture. It is important to remember that very different energies are activated in the master bedroom—such as relaxation and sensuality—and it is a good idea to create either power pots that activate both in a very balanced way or specific pots for each function that can easily change places in the house, like a rotation, to avoid excesses.

Children and Guest Bedrooms

Just like the bedroom of the couple or homeowner, the rooms where the couple's children or guests will rest also deserve special attention, and the rules for bed placement are the same as explained above. The main differences are related to *who* will use the bedroom. In a children's bedroom, for example, it is necessary to activate calm and tranquility in order to balance the excess of agitation common to childhood. In adolescence, when hormones are in full bloom, the ideal thing is to position power pots that enhance mental balance and the development of intelligence and career.

Similarly, in the guest room, we should enhance friendship, trust, and protection—both for those who use the room and for the homeowners, who receive the visitor with good intentions. However, in the case of the guest room, we should always avoid using plants that enhance leadership or the domination of ideas and favors, thus avoiding reversing the roles of host and guest.

Bathrooms and Laundry Room

The maintenance and harmonization of the energies in a home's bathrooms and laundry rooms are of fundamental importance for the flow of money and prosperity of those who live there. This is because the element of water symbolizes abundance and money, and it is precisely through the drains that water leaves the house. Furthermore, it is also there that we leave our physical and energetic dirt when washing clothes, using the toilet, and taking hygienic or magical baths. Again looking at the lessons of feng shui, Celso Yamamoto teaches us that:

> Bathrooms should not show too much, because if they are too visible, they will attract the energy of anyone who passes in front of them … If a large mirror is placed on the opposite wall of the door [the entrance to the bathroom, or on the outside of the door itself], it will reflect the hallway outside, hiding the bathroom and not attracting the vital energy of those who pass in front of it. … Painting the bathroom blue or green favors marriage and family harmony. In addition, blue and green are colors of the element of water. By painting its walls with these colors, we feed this room with the energy of its element, preventing it from absorbing the energy of other corners of the house.[37]

For this reason, it is essential to identify each of the points where water exits the house—such as drains, for example—where it is possible to place a power pot as a filter, created with cold herbs ruled mainly by the earth element, in order to neutralize this escape of energies, because earth is a complementary element to water. If it is not possible to place a pot exactly over the drain (such as the one in the shower stall), place the power pot in the nearest window or on the toilet tank.

The Backyard

The backyard of a residence, when present, acts as a protective area for those who live there. It is also considered the energetic

---

37. Yamamoto, *Feng Shui.*

"base" or "foundation" of the property. As it is the farthest point from the street—where the external energies that we cannot control can be found—it is from there that the *stability* of the house is formed. In this way, just as how in the front yard we plant species that enhance harmony, joy, happiness, prosperity, and love "from the street to the inside," in the backyard we do the same, but in the opposite direction, "from the back to the inside of the house."

The backyard is also the ideal place to plant larger trees, preferably those that bear fruit. Besides having our own orchard to delight us, the larger trees, when enchanted, will also act to support and sustain our desires, and their fruiting cycles will also work as cycles of energy renewal. Ah, cleansing is essential! Therefore, collecting the dry leaves that fall from these trees favors this renewal, and you can even use them in your fumigations!

Other Important Points

Balancing and harmonizing the energies of our home or work space goes far beyond placing our power pots at strategic points in each room. Plants have incredible magical power, but just like us, they are living beings that depend on other factors in nature to reach their best potential. So, always remember to check for and seek out the best use of the natural light that comes in through your windows, and be sure to water each pot in the right measure, according to the chosen species. Put light curtains on the windows that will allow the flow of air and energy, and—especially in the living room and kitchen—protect the exits with wind chimes or crystal pendants that will work as filters for what enters and exits through them.

Another important point, especially in rooms with less natural light, is that they are always well ventilated and that the lighting spots do not directly hit the eyes of those who frequent the room, as this can irritate both the physical and mental body. Give preference to yellowish light bulbs—they give a feeling of comfort; white light bulbs, only in the kitchen!

CHAPTER 16

The Garden of Power

Every form of affection is also a form of magic. When we smile at someone, when we say a sincere good morning, when we hug or sing, we are practicing magic. Similarly, when we dedicate our time to caring for something or someone, there too we are giving love, directing energy, and strengthening the transforming power of gratitude in our lives. With the leaves and their powers, it works the same way! The words, songs, and emotions we manifest when planting, harvesting, or handling a food or plant influence how it grows and reacts to our intentions.

Want an example? Japanese scientist Masaru Emoto did an experiment placing three portions of cooked rice in three different glass jars. On the first jar, he wrote, "Thank you, I love you." On the second, he wrote, "I hate you, you fool." On the third, he simply didn't write anything. In addition, for thirty days, he asked his students to shout at each of the jars the words written on them.

Can you imagine what the result was? At the end of the month, the rice in the first jar, with the words of affection, had begun to ferment. The rice in the second jar, with the words of bitterness, was black and rotten. And the rice in the third, without anything written on it, was all moldy. That's more proof that, as we have seen before, everything around us is potential energy, waiting to be awakened, combined, and transformed through the principle of the gift: the words, songs, and emotions that we express influence the way we live and relate to the people and the situations around us.

In addition, we have also learned that each room of the house or work space has specific energies that must be balanced and activated according to the function of each one. For this, we can use the different power pots and, whenever possible, have our own backyard with the most diverse species that we will use both in the pots that will activate the magic in our house and in creating other rituals and recipes for baths and fumigations.

Now, think with me ... If beyond the power pots it was also possible to create your own *magic garden* at home—even in small spaces, houses without a backyard, or apartments—it would be fantastic, right? And that can come true! We live in an urban environment, surrounded by buildings, asphalt, and concrete. So, I know that it is not possible for all of us to have extensive gardens or devote hours and hours a day to cultivating all the plants and flowers we would like. Still, how about creating your own magic garden at home? You don't need a lot of space, time, or investment—just good intentions.

Along with that, caring for the plants you choose reinforces their power, so select a moon phase that is good for this (waxing or full are ideal), check the energy of the day, use good quality soil, and treat them with attention and affection. Plants like to be spoiled, talked to, and hear you sing to them! In addition, many small plants (which are ideal for our home magic gardens) have a triple purpose: they can be used in bathing and fumigation rituals, in the decoration and ornamentation of your home, and also as spices while cooking (another form of magic!).

Several species of plants adapt very well to spaces with little sunlight, with high humidity, and with little need for water. Observing each of their needs, you can grow your seedlings in small pots on the balcony of your apartment or in your kitchen. Some useful and easy-to-care-for examples are:

- Rosemary
- Lemongrass and cider grass

- Coriander
- Fennel
- Mint
- Rose geranium
- Basil
- Sage
- Parsley
- Thyme

How to Create Your Magic Garden

Learning about the sacred leaves requires much more than reading and theoretical study: you have to get your hands dirty—or rather, into the earth. Feel its energy, cultivate the plants' power, and watch the magic of life growing daily before your eyes. For this reason, I created a free e-book titled *How to Create Your Magic Garden*, where you will learn the correct ways to prepare the earth, sow seeds, and take care of your plants so that they can grow strong and healthy, whether in small pots or large backyards. Access the link below and download yours!

https://www.arolecultural.com.br/magic-garden

CHAPTER 17

The Magic Kitchen

The first lesson we learn in any Afro-Brazilian spiritual tradition is that the magic of the Orishas begins in the kitchen. It is there where the sacred offerings to the deities are prepared, where sacrificed animals are cleaned after rituals, and from where the whole community eats. Each Orisha has their own particularities, their favorite foods and spices, and even those to which they are completely averse, not being able to receive them in their offerings under any circumstances.

Dr. Vilson Caetano de Souza, Jr., a researcher in the anthropology of Afro-Brazilian populations and food and culture and author of several books, among them *Comida de Santo que se Come* (*Sacred Food to be Eaten*), explains that:

> In the religions of African origin, food is understood as strength, gift, sacred energy present in the grains, roots, leaves, and fruits that spring from the earth. Food is the force that has nourished the ancestors and, at the same time, the means through which the community reaches the highest degree of intimacy with the sacred through consumption. For the people of a terreiro, informing them about the delicacies offered to the ancestors is not the same as talking about everyday eating, also called "white foods." The foods offered to the saints in the terreiros are always particular to a particular temple, although certain coherences with others can be observed. Half recipes, dishes without names, complaints, and justifications add

up to recreations, all the time, on the stove dominated by the *iabassê*, the true priestess of sacred food.[38]

In addition, food also plays a fundamental role in human health and routine: when we eat in a balanced way, our body functions correctly, and we gain more energy for everyday life; likewise, when we eat incorrectly, our body immediately reacts, and we feel tired, unwell, and even sick. With this, we can see the fundamental role of food in both its magical and physical aspects. What we often do not realize, however, is that it is possible to integrate both aspects and transform each meal into an act of magic, simply by activating the dormant power of the grains, seeds, and spices we use, based on everything we have learned so far: consciousness, purpose, words of power, and responsibility.

As we also have already seen, it is in the pantry at home that we store the food and supplies that, in the symbolism of magic, represent the abundance and prosperity of our lives. Similarly, it is in the kitchen that, when preparing any recipe, we activate the energy of the fire element more directly, through the use of the stove—and this is precisely the element that energizes our goals, "heating" the energies and allowing them to move and transform according to our wishes, acting as if it were the magical "fuel" necessary for this.

Preparing the Magic Space

Although any daily act can become a ritual of power, a magic kitchen has its particularities. The first is to create a setting that will be favorable for this environment: when deciding to prepare some magic recipe, tune the energy of the physical space to align with your goal. To do this, leave the dishes in the right

---

38. Vilson Caetano de Souza, Jr., *Comida de Santo que Se Come* (Mairiporã, Brazil: Arole Cultural, 2019).

place, clean the sink, have the stove always in order, and separate beforehand each of the ingredients and utensils that you will use in the preparation. Depending on the situation, burn some dry leaves or incense in line with the objectives of the ritual you will prepare and, if possible, take an herbal bath before you start.

An important aspect is to remember that magic happens by combining and manipulating the energies of nature. Therefore, it is always better to use utensils made of natural materials, such as metal and wood, avoiding plastic. Another thing that favors creating a magical environment in the kitchen is dedicating a few sets of wooden spoons, knives, forks, and cutting boards exclusively for magical use—but not the pans, as the more one is used, the better, since "the old pan makes good food."

Alchemy and Cooking Recipes

As you may have noticed, the art of practicing magic is very similar to the mathematical sciences: like everything in the Universe, the alchemical transformation of ingredients results from the combination of complementary pairs and, for this reason, there seem to be rules and laws that must be followed for potentiation or annulment, for union or separation, for individualization or complementation of what is desired. In a simplified way, what happens is that for a magical goal to be truly realized, it must always be *in balance*, and for this we must keep in mind that in terms of magic and energy, everything is composed of the harmonization of the four elements of nature: earth, fire, air, and water.

In addition, you can also take into consideration the way each food or ingredient is prepared when balancing the elements of nature that will make up your ritual: roasted, cooked, or fried foods always have more of the fire element, for example, while chilled or frozen foods like shakes have a much greater influence of the water element. In the same way, not every ingredient will be served: sometimes, as in teas that will be strained before drinking or in cooking sauces used on meats that will go into the oven, part of the recipe will remain "hidden," and this can be one of the great magical secrets of your recipes.

Grains, Seeds, and Flours

Every grain, seed, or flour is ruled by the element of earth and represents the potential for growth, abundance, and prosperity that has not yet been awakened. Earth is the element that also symbolizes the security of our steps, the firmness in our choices and in the paths to follow, the safety and the courage to create, and achievements. It is no wonder that the prosperity ritual made to the Orisha Oshossi always has many grains involved in its preparation.

Precisely because they symbolize abundance and growth, we need to be careful about how we store these ingredients in our kitchen or pantry. Unless you are using the grains and seeds in a power pot, it is important to always keep them away from light and moisture, in clean containers closed securely with a lid or—preferably—with a cork. First, open food jars allow dirt and insects to enter them; second, considered magically, open jars allow these ingredients' energy to drain away, taking away your prosperity.

Meat

Like any kind of pepper, from the mildest to the most intense, meats of any kind are ruled by the element of fire, especially red meat, and they represent life force, energy, and the ability to perform some action. A fundamental point that requires attention when preparing magical recipes in the kitchen is to understand the origin of the meat that will be prepared; after all, it was a life before becoming food. Considering this, what should be observed is exactly how this life was taken: there is a significant difference between *slaughter* and *sacrifice,* and this distinction makes all the difference.

It is not news that the basis of the vast majority of rituals in Candomblé and other Afro-religious traditions is animal sacrifice, which can seem scary for laypeople. The fact is that, under these conditions, an animal's life is *sacralized*—made sacred—and therefore shared between humans and gods. The animals sacrificed in these traditions must always be in perfect health and cannot suffer during the sacrificial act. Most importantly, they can only be sacrificed if they agree to surrender themselves in honor of the deities. If any of these factors are not met, the priests do not offer the animal in question; thus, meat originating from these rituals is already an element of magic in itself and can be used without further concerns. However, meat that is purchased at the supermarket mostly originates from slaughterhouses, bringing with it a lot of negative energy due to the way these animals are killed. Electric shocks, injections, and lethal blows of all sorts are the techniques commonly used by slaughterhouses, and this vibration is "recorded" in meat and blood—this is why many times when we eat meat, by the end of the meal, we feel heavy and have difficulty with digestion.

In these situations, if you do not have the option of seeking out sacrificed meats and end up having to consume slaughtered meats, it is important to release the negative energy from the food before preparing it. For this, the ideal is to wash the meat in pure water with a little coarse salt and, before the preparation, enchant it with words of power and the laying on of hands, directing the positive energies of forgiveness and love toward it. After that, you can then enchant it according to the main purpose of your ritual.

Oils and Olive Oil

Like the vast majority of aromatic herbs, vegetable oils and olive oils are ruled by the element of air. They are related to the potentialities of harmonization and balance, of aggregation, and of union; the exception is red palm oil, or *dendê*, which is ruled by the elements of fire and earth and has active potential, of generation and movement. Unlike other types of food, there are few occasions when oils are consumed alone: whether to fry, season, or finish a recipe, oils have the characteristic of being used together with other elements to enhance the flavor and aroma of the main food of the recipe we are preparing, giving a touch of sophistication to its preparation while combining their own aromas with it. It is no wonder that in Roma magic, olive oil is considered sacred and extremely powerful for "blessing" any ritual.

Powders, Spices, and Seasonings

Like vegetable oils, powders, spices, and seasonings are also collectively ruled by the element of air—although each has its own specific rules that can cover the four elements of nature. Both in cooking and in magic, powders and spices are characterized as "side dishes" to the main foods, and it is with them that we will brighten up our recipes and give them that special touch.

Milk, Eggs, and Dairy Products

Milk of different origins, eggs, and their derivatives such as cheese and butter are ruled jointly by the element of water and are, chiefly, the domain of the Iyabás—the name given to all female Orishas—and of Oshala, the father of creation. Symbols of life, multiplication, fertility, and abundance, milk and eggs are the ingredients that bind our recipes, bringing together and making each of the other items, united during the preparation, become a homogeneous whole in the final result.

Eggs have a special symbolism in magic, both energetically and biologically, since they carry within themselves a whole life. In this sense, their use has several magical functions when cooked and, in some cases, when used raw—mostly when offered to Oshun, the Orisha of fertility, beauty, and love. In turn, milk has a nutritious character, and this is the main symbolism that it also carries in its magical use: it is through milk that mothers breastfeed and give strength and health to their children.

Alternatives to milk that, besides being healthy, also have exceptional magical potentials are the vegetable milks, whether they are of natural origin, such as coconut or soy milk, or prepared at home with the different seeds and grains available.

The Benefits of Vegetable Milk

You have undoubtedly heard of them, but you may not know that there are so many of them … And I'll tell you something: there are more of them every day. Whether in home kitchens or in the recipes of renowned chefs, one thing is certain: vegetable milks are here to stay! Beyond the well-known coconut and soy milk, several other types of milk can be extracted from seeds and plants, and besides being healthy, they are also delicious!

Just like creating herbal baths and fumigations, the creation of vegetable milk can become a magical ritual. Colors, flavors, and aromas are elements that activate our senses and vibrate the energies around us. That is why you can combine the secrets and powers of the sacred leaves with recipes from the kitchen: rice for prosperity, oats for multiplication and abundance, nuts for love and seduction. When we think about our magic garden, it is clear that the main idea is to have on hand aromatic leaves and herbs to create our baths and fumigations at home—but have you ever considered using your garden as an alternative for health and quality of life?

I don't mean that you're going to plant everything you eat—after all, most of us don't live on large farms—but rethinking our eating habits and eventually replacing industrialized products with homemade or organic ones, besides being fun, can be a very healthy option. In this sense, vegetable milks are a very cool experiment that I have tested and approve of! They're also an excellent option for those who are lactose intolerant, have high cholesterol, or simply want to adopt a more balanced diet, as vegetable milks are low in fat and rich in vitamin B and iron.

The easiest vegetable milk to find in supermarkets is soy milk, which is also the most popular and most affordable. In addition to the "plain" version, several brands offer flavored soy milk or soy-based juices. Another easy-to-find option is coconut milk, which is often used to make desserts, but as time goes on it is becoming easier to find other options. Especially in the supermarkets of big cities or in specialized health-food stores, it is already possible to find, for example, affordable choices of rice milk and oat milk.

It is also possible to create and use vegetable milks from practically all types of grains and seeds—in desserts, in that snack during the day, or in sophisticated recipes, what counts here is your creativity! Their taste varies a lot from one type to another, so the thing is to experiment: if you don't like almond milk, for example, try another nut or other combinations! Just don't give up on the first try, okay?

The color of vegetable milks also varies a lot and is directly linked to the amount of ingredients, their concentration, and the combinations you create. Coconut milk and rice milk are usually the whitest; cashew milk or peanut milk are darker and cream colored. Remember that darker seeds usually have richer and more pronounced flavors; similarly, lighter-colored and softer seeds, for the most part, have more delicate flavors and blend better with each other.

Besides taste and color, nutritional properties also vary from one type of milk to another. For example, soy milk is rich in calcium and protein, rice milk in B vitamins, oat milk in vitamin E and fiber, and nut milk in omega-3 and -6 fatty acids, zinc, and minerals. Each has its own medicinal and energetic particularity, depending on the ingredients you combine, but all of them can replace animal milk in coffee, chocolate milk, vitamins, or recipes for cakes and pies.

The coolest thing about all this is that to prepare your own vegetable milk at home you need only a few utensils: a thin cloth or a fabric filter (like those sometimes used to prepare coffee); a powerful blender; pure water (preferably mineral water); and the grains or seeds you want to use. Puree everything in the blender, strain it, leave it in the refrigerator for a few minutes, and enjoy!

Fruits and Vegetables

The various type of fruits and vegetables are collectively ruled by the earth and water elements, but just like spices, they are also individually energetically related to each of the four elements of nature according to their ruling Orishas. At the same time, just like the grains and seeds, they are also always ruled by and offered to the Orisha Oshossi as a symbol of abundance, prosperity, and happiness—especially the fruits that have many seeds inside.

One of the most important things to consider when performing magic in the kitchen with fruits and vegetables—besides the energy and regency specific to each species, of course—is to observe their predominant color and shape. Those with round shapes and intense colors are often related to female Orishas and the magic of love and seduction—such as strawberries, apples, and watermelon. On the other hand, those with elongated or pointed shapes, dark colors, and strong flavors are usually related to male Orishas and the magic of protection, defense, and the opening of paths. Another fundamental issue to observe is that some Orishas and Birth Odus prefer a particular type of fruit or vegetable, but—and this is *very important*—they also have their taboos related to other species, such as, for example, Oya with pumpkin. (People under the regency of the Orisha Oya or the Odu Ossá should not even speak the name of this vegetable, calling it alternatively "red yam.") Therefore, it is always important to check if there are any restrictions regarding the Orishas that will be invoked or regarding the Birth Odu of the people involved in the ritual or to whom it is directed.

The Colors of Food in Magic

Cooking is an art and, as with all arts, it must please all the human senses: sight, smell, taste, touch, and hearing. This is because, in addition to the ingredients and incantations performed during the preparation, the personal energy of those who make the recipe and those who eat the food we prepare influences the result of the desires we command while cooking them. Let's face it, no one can keep up positive energy when coming across a dish that's assembled in an ugly or sloppy way or that smells bad, right? Therefore, the dishes' assembly and presentation are also important, as well as the care taken to balance the colors of the ingredients used so that the final result is, in addition to being magically potent, visually pleasing. With this in mind, the following list can help you choose the color of your recipes based on the goals you want to achieve. It is also worth remembering that this list of colors applies to all the elements of the ritual, from the food to the dishes or table linens you will use when serving it, the candles you use to decorate the environment, and all the other elements you will choose.

- **White:** Cleansing, protection, and peace
- **Orange:** Energy and willpower
- **Red:** Protection and sensuality
- **Yellow:** Intelligence and abundance
- **Violet:** Cleansing, protection, and evolution
- **Pink:** Love, self-esteem, and beauty
- **Light blue:** Fraternity and serenity
- **Dark blue:** Courage and prosperity
- **Green:** Physical health, money, and wisdom
- **Brown:** Security and consolidation
- **Black:** Protection, cleansing, and the end of cycles

Oh, and another thing: not all the ingredients or elements of your ritual need necessarily be edible. You can enhance your dishes with items that are purely visual or olfactory, such as using small flowers to decorate a salad or using fruit chips or aromatic roots to mix into a punch, drink, or other refreshment on hot days.

CHAPTER 18

Aromatherapy & Magic with Perfumes

Of the human body's five senses, smell is the most susceptible to the power and magic of the sacred leaves: from choosing the species we will use in our rituals to performing them, the aroma of leaves, flowers, and seeds is always a determining factor for a given plant to be a part of the magical recipes. Furthermore, smell is also the sense that can reach farther, letting us perceive a change in the environment even if we cannot see, hear, see, or touch it.

In magic, the sense of smell has been used since ancient times, when the first perfumers in history, in ancient Egypt around 2000 BC, sought to create fragrances that activated the perceptions of tranquility, sensuality, or authority by combining different scents. Nowadays, the magic of perfumes has gained a new look and has become an integral part of the list of holistic therapies through aromatherapy.

What is Aromatherapy?

Aromatherapy is a branch of holistic therapies that uses essential oils and other types of fragrances in specific applications, intending to improve the physical and emotional well-being of those who use it. In it, the different flowers, leaves, stems, roots, or seeds of plants go through extraction processes that result in highly concentrated oils that, depending on the form of application chosen, will be diluted in other oils, alcohol, or water. The therapeutic use of these applications is often confused with their magical use through the combination of aromas for their medicinal and energetic potentials. Through the activation of the senses of touch and smell, the essential oils used in aromatherapy influence the physical, mental, and spiritual bodies.

Historical Origin

Although the origin of the production of perfumes dates back to ancient Egypt around 2000 BC, it was only in the early twentieth century AD that the term *aromatherapy* and its forms of application appeared, first established by the French chemist Rene Gattefosse in his book *Aromatherapy* in 1937, in which he proposed a strictly medicinal approach to the technique. Although Gattefosse and other chemists in France, Italy, and Germany had studied the effects of aromatherapy for over thirty years, it was only in 1982 that this technique gained worldwide visibility with the book *The Practice of Aromatherapy*, by the physicist Jean Valnet.

In the 1980s and 1990s, the various techniques of holistic therapy became known worldwide, just as the traditions of magic also became more widely known in the specialized press. At the same time, with the increasing use of essential oils in medicine, several cosmetic and pharmaceutical companies created product lines based on aromatherapy, and since then, free classes and higher-level courses have been offered to the public, teaching everything from the most straightforward applications to advanced techniques and theories that combine with other alternative therapies to traditional medicine. In 2018, the Brazilian Ministry of Health included the practice of aromatherapy in the Brazilian Unified Health System, as part of the National Policy of Integrative and Complementary Practices.

Essential Oils

Essential oils are substances extracted from flowers, herbs, fruits, and spices, using different physical and chemical processes such as distillation, compression, or the use of solvents. Their use—originating in China in 2700 BC and passing through India, Arabia, Persia, and Egypt—became popular in the modern world beginning in 1563 with a publication by Giovanni Battista Della, who documented some new techniques of oil extraction, which, until then, had only been done by immersion in various types of alcohol.

In addition to their use in the food and beverage industries, cosmetics, and herbal medicine, essential oils are the basis for the application of all aromatherapy techniques. Through their extraction methods we obtain the purest extract of a plant, keeping all its physiochemical and energetic potentialities—which is why we can use them in our magical rituals.

Extraction Methods

Technological evolution has offered a series of solutions for the large-scale production of essential oils; still, it is the delicate nature of the chosen leaf and its physical characteristics in the formation of plant tissues that will determine the best technique to be used. Nowadays, there are several techniques for extracting vegetable oils, from the most rudimentary, such as vaporization and enfleurage, to cold pressing and hydrodistillation, and on to the most complex, such as extraction through the use of solvents and supercritical fluids.

When we talk about magic, it is important to remember that all the steps involved in obtaining our ingredients influence the final result of the ritual—for this reason, the more natural and pure the chosen oil, the better! However, even though it is possible to extract and make your own essential oils at home, many excellent-quality brands are available on the market, and we can hardly control which method was used in the extraction of each of them. Anyway, the most important thing in this case is to ensure that your consciousness and purpose are aligned with the goals you want to achieve with your ritual.

Steam Distillation or Vaporization

Steam distillation—also called vaporization—is the most widely used method for extracting essential oils worldwide. A simple procedure, it consists of exposing the original element to the action of steam, which passes through the plant's tissues and carries with it the oil contained in the plant's glands. The steam, now containing the oil, reaches a condenser and cools down, returning to the liquid-oily state. In the final step, the pure oil is separated from the water molecules.

Cold Pressing

Through a hydraulic press, the juice and essential oil of the manipulated plant are squeezed and extracted together, separated by water jets. After this step, the oil passes through a series of centrifuges that separate it from possible solid fragments and waste resulting from the extraction. This is the common method used to extract citrus-fruit oils such as lemon, orange, and tangerine; other oils such as almond, chestnut, and wheat oil are also extracted in this way.

Hydrodistillation

Unlike steam extraction, in which the plant matter is exposed only to vaporization, in hydrodistillation it is completely submerged in warm water (with a temperature below 100 degrees

Celsius), avoiding the cooking of the plant and the loss of its potency. From there, it flows into coils and condensers to separate the parts. It is a slow, artisanal process but is still widely used on a laboratory scale.

Enfleurage

Enfleurage, also known as enfloration, is used to extract essential oils from delicate raw materials, such as flower petals, which can have their potency lost if extracted by other methods. Developed in France in the seventeenth century, it is an extremely slow and expensive process, almost extinct nowadays; even so, of all the known methods, it is the one that provides the best quality oils and therefore has been continuously reinvented and adapted. In this technique, the petals are crushed and placed on glass plates greased with odorless animal or vegetable fat, which acts like a sponge. Every twenty-four hours, the petals are replaced, and the process is repeated for several weeks until the fat becomes saturated. From this point, it is filtered and distilled, resulting in a highly aromatic concentrate, mixed with alcohol, and distilled again, until the essential oil is obtained. In the film *Perfume: The Story of a Murderer*, based on the book of the same name, it is possible to see in detail the production of several essential oils using this technique.

Solvent Extraction

Due to their biological structure's delicate nature and sometimes because of their physiochemical characteristics, some plants cannot be subjected to the extraction processes described above, which can destroy their aromas and energetic potential. In these cases, solvent extraction is applied, and essential oils are produced by infusing these plants with chemicals such as benzene, toluene, and petroleum ether. Depending on the solvent used, the mixture that results can become extremely toxic and its purification process expensive and complicated.

Supercritical Fluids

Supercritical fluid extraction is the most complex and technological method of all, and it is also the one that produces the purest and highest quality essential oils. Along with that, this technique has gained worldwide notoriety for being a clean, nontoxic, and nonresidual technology, collaborating to preserve nature. In this type of process, the plants are exposed to gases that, at high temperature and pressure, reach a state called "supercritical," which is intermediate between liquid and gaseous. Once they reach this state, the gases can act as solvents without chemical harm, extracting the oils cleanly and purely. The biggest (and perhaps only) disadvantage of this method today is the price of the equipment needed to perform it, which on an industrial scale can run into the millions of dollars.

How to Make Essential Oils at Home

The simplest way to make essential oils at home is through extraction by natural solvents. To do so, using a dark glass bottle, simply soak about 300 grams of crushed raw plant matter in 1 liter of grain alcohol and keep it tightly closed for about thirty days, away from light and moisture. After this period, strain the mixture well and leave it in an open container, such as an agate bowl, for example, until all the alcohol evaporates and only the desired oil remains. From the very beginning, this technique can also be turned into a magic ritual, simply by including inside the bottle your requests and incantations written on virgin paper; you can also mix several ingredients and try "combined" versions of the oils.

Dangers and Cautions

Due to the high chemical concentration both of the extract itself and of the products used in its extraction, care must be taken when using essential oils—especially in direct applications on the body and skin, dilute them in water or alcohol. In an interview with *Revista Saúde* (*Health Magazine*), aromatherapist Andrea Darco—who conducts research on the medicinal application of aromatherapy at the Georges-Pompidou European Hospital in France—explains that: "Pregnant women, children under 3 years old, the elderly, epileptics, cardiac patients, people with syndromes in general, and those taking a lot of medicines should not use essential oils before undergoing a careful evaluation."[39] She also warns against the risks of using citrus oils based on orange, lemon, tangerine, or ginger. For example, applying them to the skin and then going into the sun can cause burns. In the same interview, Guilherme Peniche, a researcher at the University of São Paulo, also makes a caution: "Buy a reliable brand product, with purity certificates, and keep an eye on the essences [which are not essential oils but mixtures]: although they smell good, they do not have therapeutic properties."[40] Another aspect to be observed, in terms of magic, is that essential oils are extremely concentrated. Therefore, their use should always be done drop by drop, just as we should always remember the rules of magical balance.

---

39. Ana Luísa Moraes, "Óleos Essenciais: Usos, Descobertas … e Contraindicações," *Revista Saúde*, August 7, 2017, saude.abril.com.br /bem-estar/oleos-essenciais-usos-e-contraindicacoes.
40. Ibid.

How to Use Aromatherapy

As we have seen, the basis of aromatherapy is the essential oils and their combinations. However, there are several ways of applying these oils, which should be chosen discerningly by whoever will use them: massages, baths, compresses, inhalations, aromatizers and sprays, aromatic pillows, and foot soaks are the most well known, and each of these has specific guidelines that must be followed. In addition, when combining aromatherapy with magic, other techniques can also be used, such as the anointing of candles or other ritual elements, like poppets, for example; the "baptism" of magical artifacts or objects at home, like doorjambs; or the creation of magical perfumes for everyday use.

Massage

Massage is one of the techniques that combine several senses in a single application: besides relaxing the physical body through touch and the mental body through the creation of an environment favorable to the application and the aromas used, you can also enchant the mixture of oils for the purpose you want—for example, using them in massages to enhance sensuality and love. For this, mix 20 drops of the chosen essential oils in 30 milliliters (3 tablespoons) of extra virgin olive oil; this amount is enough for the whole body. Another option is to mix 60 drops of the oils in a 120-milliliter vegetable base or unscented lotion.

Immersion Baths

Immersion baths are an "enhanced" version of herbal baths: the mixture of oils or herbs is prepared in a bathtub, in which you immerse yourself up to the neck. The objective here, as in massage, is to activate other senses and body sensations, in addition to the magical function of the ritual. So it is recommended that, in addition to the bath recipe, you also prepare the environment in which you will perform it: lighting some candles or incense, playing background music, or adding other elements to your bath, such as flower petals or crystals, are great ideas.

The preparation of this type of bath is simple: in a standard-sized bathtub, mix 1 tablespoon of olive oil or other vegetable oil for every 5 to 10 drops of essential oil. It is recommended that you use no more than three different types of oils, as they're very concentrated and can, in high amounts, cause the skin to have allergic reactions.

Herbal Baths or Oil Baths?
As we've seen in previous chapters, in African-origin traditions such as Candomblé and Umbanda, it is very common to use herbal baths as therapeutic treatments and magic rituals. In them, the fresh leaves are boiled or macerated in pure water, mixed with the other ingredients in the recipe, strained, and then used. But ... is there any difference between using fresh leaves and essential oils for magical baths?

The answer is: *It depends.* Yes, it depends! Magic is made of symbolism and traditions, passed down from generation to generation, that obey social, cultural, energetic, and religious rules. As such, one does not work without the other. In terms of energy, both fresh leaves and essential oils have the same magical potential (as long as the oils are truly *pure*). What makes the difference, however, is the ritualistic function of the recipe being prepared: in African-origin religions, the leaves are always used in their natural form because, besides the plant magic, the power of the Orisha Ossain is invoked. Ossain is the African god of the woods, who holds dominion over and keeps the secrets of all existing plant species, and who is considered to be the leaf itself. In this case, besides the magical recipe, the tradition as well as the religious function of the ritual must be maintained, because a deity is present and fresh leaves are essential to his worship.

At the same time, when performing magical baths outside the religious context of African-origin traditions, you can prepare them using essential oils without any energetic loss. This is because essential oils are nothing less than the concentrated juice of fresh leaves and bring with them all the necessary potential. In this case, it's vital to choose wisely the origin of the oils you acquire, and to activate the power of each of them with words of power, singing to enchant.

Compresses

Compresses have a more therapeutic than magical function, as they focus on the medicinal aspects of the chosen herbs—still, you can always enchant the herbs and ingredients in use. In a liter of warm or cold water—depending on the use—mix 5 to 6 drops of essential oil, dampen a clean cloth in the mixture, and place it on the desired part of the body for fifteen to thirty minutes, repeating if necessary. Remember to take care with the concentration of the oils, due to their allergenic concerns.

Incense, Air Fresheners, and Sprays

Just like herbal baths can be replaced by essential-oil baths, so the fumigations, in some cases, can be replaced by the use of burners or warmers, natural incense, and aromatizing sprays prepared according to the herbal witchcraft tradition of the Orishas. For sprays, simply mix 3 tablespoons of grain alcohol or gin with 120 drops of the desired oils in 250 milliliters of mineral or filtered water. Mix well until a homogeneous liquid is formed, and keep it in a spray bottle away from heat and light. An interesting technique is to enhance your spray with the use of natural dyes, activating the magic of herbs and colors in a single ritual.

You can also leave some natural elements immersed in the mixture, such as cinnamon sticks or some cloves, for example.

In the case of incense bought in stores, it is important to check if it is made with dry leaves or essential oils—which will have magical power within them—or if it is simply made with regular synthetic fragrance, which will produce a good scent but has no magical potential at all.

For burners or warmers—those ceramic devices, also known as *réchauds*, that have a candle below and perfume the surroundings by heating the oils in a dish above—the measurement is 10 to 20 drops of essential oil for 1 tablespoon of filtered or mineral water. This mixture is enough for an environment of up to 20 square meters.

Inhalation

Unlike the burners and aromatizing sprays, whose main purpose is the magical and energetic harmonization of the environment, the main function of inhalation is to act on the physical body through stimuli to the central nervous system, activating biochemical connections that will then be processed by the brain, which in turn will send signals to the whole organism. This entire process happens from the inhalation of vaporized essential oils that, in microparticles, will be absorbed through the nose and by the whole respiratory system, and from there, our body will do the rest of the work. Precisely because of this, the practice of inhalation, as well as that of massages and compresses, requires specific knowledge about each of the chosen oils and their possible adverse reactions, such as a rash or allergies. Inhalation in aromatherapy is applied through vaporization and must be guided by a professional: in a container of hot water, mix 3 to 5 drops of essential oil and cover the head with a terry cloth towel, creating a kind of breathing chamber. In this process, it is essential to protect your eyes with an appropriate mask.

Aromatic Pillows

Aromatic pillows have a double function and utility, combining the energetic potentials of the burners and aromatizers with the therapeutic aspects of inhalation. Depending on the pillows' size, they can be used as decorative objects—on the sofa in the living room, for example—or placed inside your regular sleeping pillow. They also work as magical rituals, combining the power of the sacred leaves with other elements, such as the colors of the chosen fabric, the symbols embroidered on it, or the magical objects placed inside them along with the filling. As with any magical ritual, it is always important to use natural raw materials; therefore, choose carefully the type of fabric and thread that will be used in your creation, as well as the material that will fill it, giving preference to cotton, jute, or other natural fibers. Essential oils can be used to anoint the fabric and threads, or, if you prefer, you can immerse the fibers of the filling in a mixture of grain alcohol and essential oils for twenty-four hours so that they absorb the oils' energies, and then let them dry naturally until all the liquid has evaporated.

Foot Soaks

The foot soak is one of the oldest forms of relaxation and energetic remedy known to popular wisdom. Who among us has not seen or heard our grandparents recommend that we sit on the sofa and dip our feet in a tub of warm water and coarse salt at the end of a tiring day of work? Little did they know that in their wisdom, they were practicing magic.

Physically, our feet are the main point of support of the physical body; energetically and spiritually, they also serve as points of connection with the earth. For this reason, several magical traditions around the world recommend anchoring and reconnecting with nature through putting your bare feet on virgin ground. During the religious rituals of Candomblé and Umbanda, initiates in their mysteries should always go barefoot as a way to respect the deities and share energies. It is no coincidence that to prevent the flu, for example, we avoid walking barefoot: in same way that our hands are channels for imposing and directing energies, our feet are entry and exit channels of physical and magical energy. In this way, the practice of foot soaking through aromatherapy can be used both to cleanse and discharge energies and to attract and absorb them. The difference, of course, will be the herbs and essential oils chosen. Also, just as with the immersion baths and the aromatic pillows, you can include other elements in the basin used for the ritual, such as jewelry, crystals, flower petals, or horseshoes.

The preparation of a foot soak is quite simple: in an agate, stoneware, or clay bowl with 4 liters of water (hot on cold days and cool on hot days), dilute 6 drops of essential oil mixed with a spoonful of grain alcohol. Prepare your surroundings, sit back and relax, and submerge your feet in the bowl for at least one hour. Afterwards, dump the mixture out of the basin into running water, in a garden, or directly onto the earth. An important point about where to dump out the mixture after the ritual: everything in magic is symbolism and reconnection with nature. So, if you're doing a foot soak to get rid of energies, the mixture should be thrown out outside of your house; if the foot soak is to attract positivity, throw it out in your backyard or in a potted plant, never down a sink drain or toilet.

Magic Perfumery

As we have seen, the art of perfumery originated in ancient times in the Middle East, particularly in Ancient Egypt. The earliest records of the use of perfumes date back to 2000 BC, with the pharaohs and other influential members of their court. The use of perfumes gained such great importance that the first strikes in human history, in 1300 BC and 330 BC, happened when the soldiers of the pharaohs Seth I and Ramses II stopped supplying aromatic ointments. Though the methods and instruments used in the production of Egyptian perfumes were quite different from those used today, which have their origin in ninth-century Arabia, the process for extracting oil from flowers—one of the main ingredients of perfumes still today—has its origin in Persia and developed from there to Spain. The art of perfumery reached France only in the mid-twelfth and fourteenth centuries, and since then France has established itself as the European and world center for perfume research and trade.

The vast majority of the ingredients used in perfume are of plant origin, and, according to these origins and the intensity of their aromas, they are divided into seven distinct families:

- **Citrus**: Also called "fruity," their essences are extracted from the peels of fruits such as lemon, bergamot, and mandarin orange and produce light and stimulating perfumes.

- **Floral**: Extracted from flowers such as rose, violet, and jasmine, they produce soft and delicate aromas. In the composition of perfumes with floral notes, a single flower is generally used.

- **Fougère:** With a more pronounced aroma, they originate from herbaceous herbs and mixtures of alcohols, tubers, and roots, giving the perfume a raw character.

- **Chypre:** Sophisticated, the aromas of this family are extracted from mosses, generally from oak, and are reminiscent of earth.

- **Woody:** Extracted from the bark and pulp of noble trees such as pine, sandalwood, and cedar, they produce strong, almost wild aromas and have greater durability and consistency.

- **Orientals:** Exotic as the name suggests, this family is formed by extremely intense aromas, obtained from the mixture of spices such as anise, cinnamon, vanilla, cloves, and pepper.

- **Leathers:** The most intense and dry of the aromatic families, its perfumes are extracted from raw materials of vegetable and animal origin, such as tobacco, wood, and leather.

A professional perfumer can bring together three hundred different ingredients in a single recipe and has an extraordinarily sharp and well-trained sense of smell, distinguishing among more than three thousand different scents and combining them in harmony. Like a composer who writes a symphony for an orchestra, the perfumer combines different notes, and it is this mixture that results in the desired chord or harmony. More-over—and different from what most of us imagine—the duration of a perfume does not depend on fixative substances: on the contrary, its fixing is related precisely to these notes, to the concentration of the oils and extracts chosen for its mixture, to the raw materials used in its composition, and to the percentage of alcohol in which these oils and essences will be mixed. This "aromatic symphony" divides its notes and chords into three main groups:

- **Top notes (head):** This is the first impression, the one that arouses interest in the perfume; these are aromas that evaporate quickly and are felt right after spraying, such as citrus.

- **Heart notes (body):** These are the soul of the perfume, its personality, composed of notes that express the main theme that the perfume wants to pass on, evaporating more slowly and felt when it evaporates on the skin, such as floral, fougère, and orientals.

- **Base notes (base):** The last chord to be perceived in the aromatic symphony of a perfume, it is responsible for fixing the fragrance, and it evaporates slowly, such as woody, leathers, and chypre.

The choice of ingredients and the composition of notes will form the final fragrances of perfumes made around the world. However, it is still necessary to observe the concentration of its aromatic oils in relation to the base liquid—called the *vehicle*—that will compose the final recipe, usually a mixture of grain alcohol and water. Standard to the perfume industry, four scales of oil concentration and mixture are used, namely:

- **Eau Fraiche (scented water):** A more diluted version of the fragrance, with 1 to 3 percent perfume oil in alcohol and water, this lasts less than an hour.

- **Eau de Cologne (cologne):** The oldest expression used to define a perfume, it is composed of 2 to 4 percent perfume oil in alcohol and water, lasting an average of two hours.

- **Eau de Toilette (bath water):** The most commonly found formula in the perfume trade is composed of 5 to 15 percent perfume essence dissolved in alcohol and lasts about three hours.

- **Eau de Parfum (perfume):** The most concentrated and long-lasting of the mixtures, it contains 15 to 20 percent pure perfume essence and lasts from five to eight hours.

With these basic concepts of perfume creation, you can prepare your perfumes in the right way. For this, besides choosing the oils and fragrances based on their specific magical potentials, it is also fundamental to remember the rules of magical balance and inequality. Observe carefully your goal for the perfume you are creating—to attract or ward off, to activate or neutralize, to soothe or provoke—and from there define the number of ingredients you will use. At the same time, remember that everything in the Universe happens from the *balance* of energies, and therefore for every hot and active ingredient, we must match another to calm it down.

As with all the rituals we have learned so far, it is important to create a favorable environment for the production of your recipe, choose the correct moon phase, and pronounce the specific incantations to awaken the power of each leaf or oil you use. Similarly, as we have already done with the power pots and aromatic pillows, you can also write your enchantments and wishes on a blank sheet of paper and put it inside your bottle of perfume!

How to Create Your Magic Perfume

Once you have learned the basics to compose your aromatic symphony and have observed the magical precepts to choose the ingredients for your recipe and balance them through the fundamentals of magical balance and inequality, it is time to create your magic perfume. The preparation of this type of ritual is very simple, and for this you will need:

- 1 large dark glass bottle for preparation (can be a common beer bottle)
- 1 glass spray bottle with a capacity of at least 100 milliliters
- 1 medium funnel that will fit in the spray bottle
- 40 milliliters of grain alcohol
- 40 milliliters of distilled water
- 20 milliliters of the chosen essential oils

Two important observations: (1) the 20 milliliters of oils correspond to the total of them, already mixed according to your magic recipe; (2) if you do not want to use distilled water, make your mixture in the proportion of 80 milliliters of grain alcohol to 20 milliliters of oils. Distilled water and grain alcohol can easily be found in specialized pharmacies.

With all the necessary items organized, using the funnel, pour the water and alcohol into the dark glass bottle and, one by one, mix with the chosen essential oils, pronouncing their incantations. Cap the bottle and store it in the refrigerator for seven days. After this period, strain the mixture and transfer the contents into the spray bottle, and that's it! If you like, you can also add magical elements to the initial mixture, such as bark, roots, coins, or crystals.

CHAPTER 19

Other Rituals of Magic with Herbs

In addition to the magic of the baths and fumigations we learned about at the beginning of the book, through the ancient foundations of the religion of the Orishas and the lessons on balancing and nourishing the energies of our homes and our physical, mental, and spiritual bodies, other forms of magic from various traditions around the world can also be easily performed at home and used to harmonize the vibrations of the environment around us and favor our goals—from the most common to the most complex. In all of them, it is always worth remembering the basic concepts of energy manipulation—*responsibility, awareness, and purpose.* Add to these all the other lessons in our journey with the sacred leaves and, I'm sure, you will transform every little act of your day into a powerful ritual!

Bed of Leaves

Another very common magic technique in the initiation rituals of Candomblé and in the energetic and medicinal treatments of shamans is the bed of leaves. In this type of ritual, in addition to the magical and therapeutic potential of lying on sacred herbs, you can also combine practices such as guided meditation or yoga, for example. The assembly of a bed of leaves is very easy: having selected the necessary plants, place them one by one on the floor, making a kind of bed. The smaller leaves should always go first, covered by the larger leaves like a natural blanket; when finishing, on top of everything else, place a straw mat where you will lie down for a while. A very important aspect in performing this type of ritual is to know the vibration of each of the chosen species: hot leaves should *never* be positioned near your head, because the energy of these herbs is too strong and can be harmful to mental balance. Likewise, avoid putting very cold leaves near your feet, so that your paths are always active and dynamic.

Sweat Lodges and Steam Tents

Steam tents are typically indigenous rituals and are widely used today in shamanic traditions around the world. However, care must be taken if you do not have experience with this type of practice, because the chemical potential of some herbs may cause poisoning and other physical ailments. Setting up a sweat lodge is complicated and, in its original form, will require you to build a tent or hut big enough to accommodate you safely; after all, inside it you will also light coals that will heat a pile of stones until it gets hot enough to evaporate the mixture of water and essential oils poured over them. My advice? Don't try this kind of ritual at home without the accompaniment of people experienced in it! An alternative is to adapt this same technique to saunas: prepare a mixture of 1 liter of distilled water with 60 to 100 drops of essential oils and gradually pour this mixture over the sauna's stones so that it evaporates.

Wreaths and Arrangements

Like shamanic sticks and power pots, plant arrangements and wreaths have a dual function—magical and decorative—and follow the same assembly and enchantment principles we learned earlier. The main difference in this case is that their shape also has magical symbolism. In the case of wreaths, because of their circular shape, the ideal is to create combinations of herbs for attraction, generation, and enhancement. Magically, the circle is a symbol of infinity and continuity, as it is not possible to identify either its beginning or its end; it also represents the womb, the potential for the generation of life and multiplication. For this reason, even when including cruder elements in their making, wreaths should be prepared and enchanted as *talismans* (magical artifacts that attract our desires) and not as *amulets* (artifacts that drive away negativities). On the other hand, arrangements can be enchanted for both functions, talisman or amulet. Remember, however, that shape and color are important magical aspects when assembling them.

Roma Pots

Roma pots are another way to use sacred leaves, flowers, herbs, and seeds in your magic rituals while decorating your home or altar. By the way, one of the main aspects of any Roma magic ritual is the beauty of what you see and don't see: colors, shapes, scents, sparkles … everything in Roma magic is always created with whimsy and with a careful aesthetic, even when they must be hidden from prying eyes, such as, for example, the magnetism pots of the Roma Guardians, which should not be exposed to naked eyes.

Like the power pots, Roma pots can be created and enchanted for all kinds of purposes, be it attraction, protection, sensuality, health, or energetic and physical defense. In each case, a wide variety of grains, seeds, and spices will be chosen and enchanted, as well as magical artifacts such as crests and coins, various perfumes, earth from several locations, and so on. Also, Roma magic is directly related to the elements of nature, the seasons, and the moon phases, which must be carefully observed when performing its rituals.

Another important element when creating Roma pots is the material and shape of the chosen pot or vase. One whose purpose is to attract a particular type of energy should be made of glass, have a height greater than its length, and have a wide mouth, which allows the circulation of the energies stored there. On the other hand, Roma pots that seek to establish, consolidate, and maintain a certain magical objective must be longer than their height. If they are related to the elements of water or air, they must be made of glass; those related to the elements of earth or fire must be made of stoneware or clay.

Similarly, the main purpose for which the Roma pot is created is what will determine whether it should be kept open or closed. Pots created to attract energies should always be open and preferably be "crowned" with one or more magnets. On the other hand, pots to collect and anchor energies should be kept closed—if they are glass, with cork stopper, and if they are stoneware or clay, with the material from which they are made. This reasoning is also used when defining the order of the ingredients that will be placed in your Roma pots. Generally speaking, warmer herbs, spices, and magical artifacts (usually in darker colors) should be placed at the bottom, while the cooler ones (in lighter colors) should be at the top of the pot. However, this order can be applied in reverse when we are seeking to anchor or ground a certain vibration.

In addition, the magic of the Roma pots tells a story, grows, and flourishes in the eyes of those who see them. Therefore, the ingredients used in their making should not simply be mixed and placed inside them; rather, they should be assembled in layers, one for each grain, leaf, or magical artifact. Between each layer, besides verbalizing your incantations, you can also place your written requests and wishes, anointing each one with specific essential oils or with olive oil—a sacred element for the

Roma people, one which symbolizes wealth, happiness, and connection between the divine and the profane. In the rest of the chapter, you will find a list of the magical elements and artifacts that I commonly use to compose my rituals and that can be used in your Roma pots, power pots, and other recipes. Enjoy!

Magical Objects and Artifacts

As we have seen, every magic ritual, in any tradition throughout the world, is made up of symbolism and combinations. Of course, the simplest rituals have their power with only one or a few elements! Still, the practice of magic activates several visible and invisible aspects and is always related to the fundamental balance between the four elements of nature—earth, fire, air, and water—and the three bodies that make up each of us—physical, mental, and spiritual. So, when we perform a ritual, we are symbolically replicating in it the entire Universe, so that, through the gift, we can reach our goals.

Besides leaves, fruits, seeds, grains, and roots, different objects and artifacts of natural origin—and also some created by humans—have vibration and magical potential that we can add to our recipes. For this, we just need to know a little more about their meanings and symbolisms, combining each of them as if telling a story or playing a symphony so that, by enchanting them, they assume specific functions and fulfill our wishes in a harmonious and balanced way.

Crystals and Precious Stones

Crystals and precious and semi-precious stones are the best-known elements of magic. Collectively ruled by the earth element, each of them has its own physical characteristics and energetic regencies, and therefore it is recommended that you study them before using their powers in rituals. In general terms, they symbolize beauty, wealth, and vitality; however, the shape, texture, color, transparency, and origin of each crystal or stone influence its magical meanings.

Jewelry and Coins

From ancient times until today, jewelry made of different metals and stones has symbolized beauty, power, material wealth, and often authority. It is no wonder that kings and queens wear their crowns, necklaces, and bracelets with stateliness when they appear in public. Moreover, the metals with which they are made also have their specific powers, and the more noble the material used—such as gold and silver, for example—the greater the magical power attached to them.

Coins, in turn, besides symbolizing prosperity, are also related to the opening of paths, to the ability to exchange and obtain gains and advantages, and to movement and multiplication—regardless of the monetary value they represent. This means that both a dollar coin and a penny have the same magical value, just like old and new coins: the idea is that a dollar coin used only once was worth only a dollar during its whole existence, while a ten-cent coin that was used a thousand times was worth much more! An important aspect of this symbolism concerns foreign coins: in addition to the meanings already explained, they also represent cultural plurality and the possibility of seeking and conquering new horizons and goals.

Utensils, Pots, Bowls, and Cauldrons

Wooden forks and spoons—phallic in shape and therefore male artifacts—as well as copper and bronze pots, wooden bowls, and iron cauldrons—which resemble the uterus and are therefore considered female artifacts—are magical objects that represent the generation and maintenance of life and, therefore, prosperity and abundance. Their use should always follow the principles of energy balance, the marriage of vibrations so that goals are achieved in harmony. In this way, the forks and spoons—or even, in European witchcraft traditions, the ritual daggers called *athames*—symbolically fertilize the pots, bowls, and cauldrons, which can be used as containers for preparing liquids and potions during rituals or as a basis for power pots and Roma pots. Also, wooden spoons especially contain symbolism related to the feeding and sustenance of the community for which the ritual is intended, be it a larger group of people—such as a work collective or a company—or members of a family.

Magnets

The symbolism of magnets is quite obvious: to attract, to gather, to bring close. Their application, however, must observe the shape and size of the magnet used: in the form of a hollow circle, a coin, or a horseshoe. Magnets can be used inside power pots or Roma pots: for example, as dividers between one layer and another. Another common use is in poppets and in spells for love and relationships.

Horseshoes

Horseshoes, along with crystals, are perhaps the best-known elements of magic. Who has not heard of putting a horseshoe above a door to attract good luck, for example? Made from cast iron by the hard work of blacksmiths, horseshoes are considered artifacts of male energy and therefore of active energy, ruled by the element of fire and the Orisha Ogun.

Their energetic potential is related to movement, advancement and progress, intelligence, and good luck—and the more they are used, the better. Their use is very common in Roma magic, where the position in which a horseshoe is used makes all the difference: turned upward, it becomes a kind of lightning rod for the desired energies; when downward-facing, it directs and anchors these energies in the location where it is placed.

Keys

Keys are magical artifacts with various symbolisms, depending mainly on their origin, size, and the position in which they are used in our rituals. Generally, they are ruled by the fire element, symbolizing the phallus, and are related to the ability to open and close paths, allow movement or prevent change, reveal secrets, or keep and hide what is desired. In addition, because they are the ones who open and close the doors of the house, they are also related to protection and guarding what is important to us.

In the Afro-religious tradition called Batuque, widespread in southern Brazil, keys are the ultimate symbol of the Orisha Bará—also called Eshu, the lord of paths and possibilities. In the dances performed in honor of this Orisha, worshippers move their hands from one side to the other, as if carrying a key and, with it, opening the space in front of them.

Batuque also teaches us how to position keys for one or another objective: crossed upward and positioned with the "secret" (tumblers) facing out, they symbolize growth and expansion; crossed upward with the secret facing inside, they represent attraction and union; pointed downward with the secret facing inside, they symbolize protection and furnishing; pointed downward with the secret facing out, they represent the release of what is kept, the revelation of what had been hidden.

Horns

Like keys, the horn of any animal symbolizes the phallus, the male element that generates life and, therefore, that multiplies and reproduces. However, because they are of animal origin, horns are governed by the element earth, and in Candomblé and Umbanda traditions, they are always related to the Orisha Oshossi. Furthermore, in many cultures worldwide, horns were also everyday utensils, used as cups and bowls or as pots. With the tip of the horn facing upward, it is used actively, for attraction; lying down, it represents balance; with the tip of the horn turned downward, it is used passively, for expansion. Another use of horns—especially those of ox or buffalo—is to hide what's inside.

Screws and Train Tracks

Other magical artifacts related to active and male energetic potentials are screws and train tracks, ruled by the fire element and the Orisha Ogun, just like horseshoes. Yet, unlike them, screws and rails—besides symbolizing technology, progress, and movement—are directly related to the anchoring and stabilization of the energies invoked, to the grounding and consolidation of the enchantment. In the case of screws, when facing upwards they can also serve as energy lightning rods, just like horseshoes and the knives and spears that we will see later. Pointing downward, they fasten and group together the other elements of the ritual, providing security and firmness, uniting them physically and magically. Rails, in turn, can also be used in directing energy, creating a barrier of protection and solidity when creating a power garden, for example. Buried at the house's main entrance gate, they also protect against theft and robbery and favor the leadership of the person who performs the ritual.

Feathers and Plumes

In contrast to keys, horseshoes, screws, and horns, the feathers and plumes of various living birds are considered artifacts of female energy, ruled by the air element and the Orisha Oshun. Depending on the animal from which they're taken, they can be applied both in cleansing and spiritual discharge spells, as well as in love, fertility, prosperity, and openness spells—to choose the right one, it is worth observing how the animal in question eats and lives. In addition, feathers and plumes symbolize the ability to move, to flow, and to direct our desires. Their colors and textures should also be considered in the composition of your rituals, as should the way they were obtained—always after the animal's natural or sacrificial death, never by slaughter.

Mirrors

Like feathers and plumes, mirrors are magical artifacts of female energy, but they are ruled by the water element and the Orishas Oshun and Yemaya. Their magical potentials are related to beauty and fertility, expansion and multiplication, and how we wish to direct energies into or out of the environment. Mirrors of any size and shape are excellent defenses against envy and the evil eye, especially when combined with herbs and crystals for this same purpose. Also, some witchcraft traditions use mirrors as an artifact of divination, opening portals through them to communicate with deities and the spirits of the dead.

An important aspect in the use of mirrors, which is widely used in feng shui and which can be used both in the decoration and creation of your Roma pots and power pots, is the shape of the piece chosen: flat, concave, or convex. The flat mirror, which is the most common, has a neutral action and can be activated according to the desired enchantments. Concave mirrors (with the shape of the letter C and with the reflecting part inside the curve) should be used to reduce or remove the energies they reflect. In contrast, convex mirrors (with the shape of the letter C but with the reflective part on the *outside* of the curve) are used to attract, amplify, and bring closer what is desired.

Nails, Spears, Knives, and Scissors

Of all the magical elements and artifacts mentioned so far, nails, knives, and spears are the only ones that have dubious symbolism, serving for both defense and attack. With a phallic form and thus of active and male energy, the use of these artifacts must be done with discretion so that they do not "overheat" their recipes, harming the rituals by attracting aggressive vibrations.

Spears are the most suitable elements to use as receptors of negative energy, and they should always be planted in the ground to neutralize any vibrations they may absorb. When placed diagonally, they have a warlike character; when placed perpendicular to the ground, with the spear point upward, they serve as energy receptors.

In the specific case of knives and scissors, as well as blades and razors of all kinds, their energies are activated to cut, divide, or separate. For this reason, popular wisdom teaches that it is bad luck to keep opening and closing a pair of scissors in the air, because this act can cut the victories that are on our path. In Roma magic, a knife that falls on the ground attracts fights and confusion, and if this happens, one should immediately pick it up and, with the tip, scratch the floor three times in the shape of a cross.

Further, the material from which these artifacts are made will define the magical objectives for which they are intended: those made of iron or metal alloy are ruled by the fire element and, as we have already seen, can be used for attack, defense, and protection. Those that are made of bones or horns, which are ruled by the earth element, are related to hunting, feeding, the daily battle for the achievement of goals, and survival in the face of the dangers and challenges of everyday life.

PART TWO

Dictionary of Magical Herbs

Dictionary of Magical Herbs

S ince ancient times, nature has served as a source of knowledge, sustenance, and healing for all humanity. Magical and
religious traditions all over the world make use of its elements
with the most varied symbolisms, as well as enjoying its properties and secrets. Earth, fire, air, and water emerge as the starting
point for the creation of recipes for healing the body and soul,
for transforming, and for manipulating reality to conquer our
deepest desires. In addition, fauna and flora have also been inspiration for the arts, medicine, and technology over the centuries.

The Brazilian flora, in particular, draws attention for its plurality: the most powerful in the medical and pharmaceutical
industries look to us and, for decades, have unveiled the healing
properties of the various natural species found in our country.
However, science leaves aside the metaphysical character of these
species, and their secrets end up being lost in time, erasing knowledge of paramount importance for us to, finally, be able to recon-
nect with the Sacred—whatever its name and form may be.

In the previous chapters of *Sacred Leaves*, you have learned
techniques on how to combine and balance plants' powers to
create magic recipes and rituals, how to identify and classify
them within the rules of magic, and how to balance their ingredients. From now on, it's time to put into practice everything
you've learned!

The content you will see now is an attempt to rescue and
record part of the sacred knowledge left by those who came
before us and who, through their wisdom, allowed life to develop
until the present. The following list of herbs and plants works like
a dictionary, with 365 species described by their specific properties

and powers and organized according to their magical classification parameters: ruling Orisha, element of nature, energy, and vibration. From this information and knowledge on how to combine and balance them through the concept of magical inequality, you will be able to carry out your experiments with confidence and security, seeking and achieving your goals with the use of magical baths, fumigations, soaps, powders and more!

The plants in this list are arranged alphabetically by the most commonly known popular name in English; occasionally, there is no English term for the species, and in these cases the local Brazilian name is given. This is followed by other popular names if available and, always, the scientific names of each plant—which are also, in some cases, followed by other scientific names of related species. In the same way, the names in the Yoruba language of each species are given, so that you can use them in the creation of incantations and songs to awaken the powers of each leaf—the *ofós*—or even so that you can substitute for them by comparing their scientific and liturgical names. After all, we have already learned that *many names carry many powers!*

Abiu

Lucuma caimito, Pouteria caimito

Liturgical Names: Osàn Olómo Wéwé, Osàn Palambí, Osàn Àgbàlùmò, Osàn Èdùn, Osànko, Àgbàlùmó Olómo

Ruling Orishas: Oshala, Oshun
Elements of Nature: Air, Water
Magical classification: Female/Passive

Helps overcome relationship breakdowns; brings strength and courage to face challenges.

Abre-caminho ("Open-path" fern)

Lygodium volubile

Liturgical Name: Ewé Lorogún
Ruling Orisha: Ogun
Element of Nature: Earth

Magical Classification: Male/Active

Opens paths; attracts good energies; strengthens leadership instincts.

Absinthe

Other Popular Names: Losna, wormwood
Artemisia absinthium

Ruling Orisha: Ogun
Element of Nature: Earth

Magical Classification: Male/Active

Attracts harmony, peace, and peaceful thoughts; excellent in the spiritual purification of the body and surroundings; favors clairvoyance and love; strengthens friendships and social relationships.

Acacia

Moringa oleifera

Liturgical Name: Ewé Ilé
Ruling Orishas: Oshossi
Element of Nature: Earth

Magical Classification: Male/Active

Helps in the treatment of insomnia and anxiety; protects against nightmares.

Açoita-cavalo ("Horse-whip" tree)

Luehea speciosa

Ruling Orishas: Ogun
Element of Nature: Earth

Magical Classification: Male/Active

Helps to overcome the pain of loss and death; combats sadness and melancholy; has extraordinary effects on discharging and shaking-off baths.

African baobab
Adansonia digitata
Liturgical Name: Igi Osé
Ruling Orishas: Iroco, Oshala, Shango
Elements of Nature: Air, Fire
Magical Classification: Female / Passive

It is considered one of the creation trees, and its leaves give longevity and dignity to those who use them.

African basil
Other Popular Names: Clove basil, alfavaca-de-cobra
Ocimum gratissimum l.
Liturgical Name: Efinrin
Ruling Orisha: Oshossi
Element of Nature: Earth
Magical Classification: Male / Active

Used in cleaning or spiritual discharge recipes.

African mahogany
Khaya grandifoliola, Khaya ivorensis
Liturgical Names: Apáòká, Ògànwó
Ruling Orisha: Oshossi
Element of Nature: Earth
Magical Classification: Male / Active

It is the home of the great ancestral mothers and is used as a catalyst for protection and defense.

African oil palm
Other popular name: Dendezeiro
Elaeis guineensis
Liturgical Names: Màrìwò, Igi Opè
Ruling Orishas: Eshu, Ogun
Elements of Nature: Earth, Fire
Magical Classification: Male / Active

Opens paths; attracts good energies; strengthens mediumship and spirituality; brings strength and courage to face challenges.

Akoko

Other Popular Names: African border tree, boundary tree
Newbouldia laevis

Liturgical Name: Akóko
Ruling Orishas: Oshossi
Element of Nature: Earth

Magical Classification: Male /
Active

Attracts prosperity; facilitates facing the challenges of destiny; obtains favors and makes opinions heard and accepted; it is the royalty leaf, being used to obtain honors and titles.

Alecrim-de-tabuleiro ("Rosemary-of-tray")

Lippia gracilis

Liturgical Name: Efinrin
Ruling Orisha: Oshala
Element of Nature: Air

Magical Classification: Female /
Passive

Used in recipes for spiritual discharging and cleansing.

Alexandrian senna

Other popular name: Cassia
Cassia acutifolia, Cassia angustifolia

Ruling Orishas: Omolu, Oshala
Element of Nature: Air, Earth

Magical Classification: Male /
Active

Attracts harmony, peace, and peaceful thoughts; strengthens friendships and social relationships; improves the ability to speak in public and make speeches.

Allamanda

Other popular name: Golden trumpet
Allamanda

Ruling Orisha: Omolu
Element of Nature: Earth

Magical Classification: Male /
Active

Used for spiritual cleansing and discharging.

Almond

Other popular name: Brazil nut
Bertholletia excelsa, Terminalia glaucescens

Liturgical Names: Irú Èkùró
Òyìnbó Kan
Ruling Orisha: Eshu
Element of Nature: Fire

Magical Classification: Male /
Active

Attracts money, prosperity, and wisdom; its branches, hanging at a shop's entrance, attract profitable customers.

Aloe

Other Popular Names: Aloe vera, torch aloe
Aloe arborescens, Aloe vera

Liturgical Names: Ipè Erin, Ipòlerin
Ruling Orishas: Eshu, Omolu, Oshala

Element of Nature: Air, Earth
Magical Classification: Male / Active

Attracts love and beauty; it favors sympathy and recognition.

Amazon water lily

Other Popular Name: Royal water lily
Victoria amazonica

Liturgical Names: Ewé Omi Ojú, Òsíbàtá
Ruling Orishas: Iyewa, Oshun

Element of Nature: Water
Magical Classification: Female / Passive

Attracts love and seduction; gives eloquence to words; strengthens mediumship and spirituality, especially when used together with the herb of Santa Luzia; brings recognition and personal brilliance.

American beech

Fagus grandifolia

Ruling Orisha: Logunede
Element of Nature: Water

Magical Classification: Female / Passive

Increases creativity and inspiration; excellent for activating the artistic potential of things and people.

American muskwood

Other Popular Name: Bilreiro
Guarea guidonia

Liturgical Name: Ìpèsán
Ruling Orisha: Shango
Element of Nature: Fire

Magical Classification: Male / Active

It is excellent to ward off negative energies that interfere with magic rituals; strengthens mediumship and spirituality; turns hatred, anger, and fury into fuel so that we can fight the injustices of the world wisely.

Angelica

Angelica archangelica, Polianthes tuberosa

Ruling Orisha: Oshala

Element of Nature: Air

Magical Classification: Female/
Passive

Promotes health, clairvoyance, and spiritual development; provides loving connections in the magic of love.

Angelim-amargoso

Other Popular Name: Morcegueira
Andira anthelmia

Ruling Orishas: Eshu, Nana

Elements of Nature: Fire, Water

Magical Classification: Female/
Passive

Used in recipes for discharging and spiritual cleansing.

Apple

Malus domestica

Liturgical Names: Èso Òro
Òyìnbó

Ruling Orishas: Iansã, Obba,
Oshun

Element of Nature: Water

Magical Classification: Female/
Passive

Consolidates desires; excellent in love spells.

Apple blossom

Malus domestica

Ruling Orisha: Oshun

Element of Nature: Water

Magical Classification: Female/
Passive

Wards off panic; acts on the consolidation of love and friendships; increases security and self-confidence.

Apricot

Prunus armeniaca

Liturgical Names: Èso Òyìnbó
Kan

Ruling Orishas: Oshun, Oshossi

Elements of Nature: Earth,
Water

Magical Classification: Male/
Active

Opens paths; attracts prosperity, abundance, and plenty; attracts good energies; strengthens the instincts of leadership; and brings brightness and personal recognition.

Araçá

Psidium araça

Liturgical Name: Gurofá
Ruling Orishas: Oshala, Oshossi
Elements of Nature: Air, Earth

Magical Classification: Male / Active

Used in recipes for spiritual purification.

Arapoca-branca

Neoraputia alba

Ruling Orisha: Oshun
Element of Nature: Water

Magical Classification: Female / Passive

Excellent to break and ward off envy and intrigue.

Areca palm

Other Popular Names: Butterfly palm, golden cane palm
Dypsis lutescens

Ruling Orishas: Eshu, Ogun
Elements of Nature: Fire, Earth

Magical Classification: Male / Active

Protects the entrances of houses, shops, and temples against negative energies and malicious people.

Argentine cedar

Cedrela brasiliensis

Liturgical Name: Òpepe
Ruling Orisha: Nana
Element of Nature: Water

Magical Classification: Female / Passive

Strengthens spirituality and connection with the sacred.

Aridan

Tetrapleura tetraptera

Liturgical Name: Arìdan
Ruling Orishas: Eshu, Oshun, Shango

Element of Nature: Fire
Magical Classification: Male / Active

Opens paths; excellent in cases of justice, documents, and contracts; facilitates learning and improves the ability to learn; makes wishes fulfilled; strengthens and attracts love, passion, and beauty.

Arnica

Other Popular Names: Wedelia, creeping daisy
Wedelia paludosa

Liturgical Name: Tamandi   **Magical Classification:** Male /
Ruling Orishas: Ogun, Oshun   Active
Element of Nature: Fire

Opens the channels of spiritual communication and clairvoyance.

Arrowleaf sida

Sida rhombifolia

Liturgical Name: Àsaragogó   **Magical Classification:** Male /
Ruling Orisha: Eshu   Active
Element of Nature: Fire

Used in recipes for discharge and spiritual cleansing.

Artichoke

Cynara scolymus

Ruling Orisha: Iansã   **Magical Classification:** Female /
Element of Nature: Fire   Passive

Helps overcome relationship breakdowns.

Asafoetida

Ferula assa-foetida

Ruling Orisha: Eshu   **Magical Classification:** Male /
Element of Nature: Fire   Active

Used in recipes for unloading and spiritual cleansing.

Ash tree

Other Popular Names: Common ash, European ash

Ruling Orisha: Oshun   **Magical Classification:** Female /
Element of Nature: Water   Passive

Attracts prosperity and spiritual protection; strengthens mediumship
and spirituality.

Assa-peixe

Vernonia polysphaera
Liturgical Name: Ewé Ewúúro
Ruling Orishas: Yemaya, Nana, Omolu
Elements of Nature: Earth, Water
Magical Classification: Male / Active

Used in recipes for spiritual discharging.

Atori

Other Popular Name: Guaxima
Glyphaea brevis
Liturgical Name: Àtòrì
Ruling Orishas: Oshossi, Omolu
Element of Nature: Earth
Magical Classification: Male / Active

Used in recipes for spiritual discharging.

Bamboo

Bambusa vulgaris
Liturgical Name: Apákò
Ruling Orisha: Iansã
Element of Nature: Air
Magical Classification: Female / Passive

It prevents fights between two people; it is the leaf that gives long life and resistance to the storms of fate.

Barbados gooseberry

Other Popular Name: Leaf cactus
Pereskia aculeata
Ruling Orisha: Eshu
Element of Nature: Fire
Magical Classification: Male / Active

Used in recipes for discharge and spiritual cleansing.

Barbatimão

Stryphnodendron
Ruling Orishas: Iyewa, Oshun, Oshumare
Element of Nature: Water
Magical Classification: Female / Passive

Opens channels of spiritual communication and clairvoyance.

Basil

Ocimum americanum, Ocimum minimum

Liturgical Names: Efinrin Wewe, Efinrín, Efinrín Kékeré

Ruling Orishas: Yemaya, Oshala

Elements of Nature: Water, Air

Magical Classification: Female / Passive

Attracts good luck and happiness; favors love and friendships; brings purification and spiritual protection.

Bay laurel

Other Popular Names: Bay leaf, sweet bay
Laurus nobilis

Liturgical Name: Ewé Asá

Ruling Orishas: Iansã, Oshala, Oshossi

Element of Nature: Earth

Magical Classification: Male / Active

Opens the paths of abundance and prosperity; excellent for attracting financial resources; favors business and brings professional success; strengthens spirituality and mediumship; symbolizes victory and recognition.

Bayhops

Ipomoea pes-caprae

Liturgical Name: Irú Ohun Ògbìn Kan

Ruling Orisha: Oshossi

Element of Nature: Earth

Magical classification: Male / Active

Attracts prosperity, abundance, and plentifulness.

Belladonna

Other popular name: Deadly nightshade
Atropa belladona

Ruling Orisha: Eshu

Element of Nature: Fire

Magical Classification: Male / Active

Attracts money, prosperity, and wisdom; its branches should be hung on ash trees at the entrances of commercial establishments to attract profitable customers; used in strong discharge baths to destroy negative fluids.

Belladonna lily

Amaryllis beladona

Liturgical Name: Àlùbósà   **Magical Classification:** Male/
Ruling Orishas: Eshu, Omolu   Active
Elements of Nature: Fire, Earth

Used in recipes for discharging and spiritual cleansing.

Bellyache bush

Other Popular Name: Cotton-leaf physic nut
Jatropha gossypifolia

Liturgical Name: Bòtújè Pupa   **Magical Classification:** Male/
Ruling Orisha: Eshu   Active
Element of Nature: Fire

Used in recipes for discharging and spiritual cleansing.

Benjamin fig

Ficus benjamina

Liturgical Name: Èso Òpòtó   **Magical Classification:** Male/
Ruling Orishas: Eshu, Omolu   Active
Elements of Nature: Fire, Earth

Used in recipes for discharging and spiritual cleansing.

Benzoin

Stryrax benjoin

Ruling Orishas: Oshala, Oshun   **Magical Classification:** Female/
Elements of Nature: Air, Water   Passive

Attracts positive energies, fights negative energies, and purifies the environment; increases creativity, whether in art or written works; eliminates spiritual blocks; harmonizes our reasoning.

Betis-branco

Piper rivinoides

Liturgical Name: Ewé Boyí   **Elements of Nature:** Air, Water
Funfun   **Magical Classification:** Female/
Ruling Orishas: Yemaya, Oshala   Passive

Attracts harmony, peace, and peaceful thoughts; excellent in the spiritual purification of the body and surroundings; strengthens friendships and social relationships.

Birch

Betula alba, Betula pendula
Ruling Orishas: Iansã, Oshun   **Magical Classification:** Male/
Element of Nature: Fire   Active

Consolidates desires; strengthens and attracts love and passion.

Birthwort

Aristolochia clematitis, Aristolochia gigantea
Liturgical Names: Jókónijé,   **Elements of Nature:** Air, Water
Àkónijé   **Magical Classification:** Female/
Ruling Orishas: Oshala, Oshun   Passive

Calms and "settles" the energies in a specific place, holds people in the same place, and avoids wanderings.

Bitter kola

Other Popular Name: Orogbo
Garcinia kola
Liturgical Name: Orógbó   **Magical Classification:** Male/
Ruling Orisha: Shango   Active
Element of Nature: Fire

Helps in dreams of premonition and in contact with ancestors; considered the seed that makes one become a king; teaches that forgiveness is the way to happiness; makes you find what is lost.

Bitter melon

Momordica charantia l.
Liturgical Names: Wéwé, Èjìnrìn   **Elements of Nature:** Earth, Fire
Ruling Orishas: Oshumare,   **Magical Classification:** Male/
Shango, Nana   Active

In the regency of Nana, it is related to the funeral rituals of Candomblé; excellent for attracting prosperity, good deals, and honorifics.

Bitter orange

Citrus aurantium
Liturgical Name: Òrombó   **Element of Nature:** Fire
Gaingain   **Magical Classification:** Male/
Ruling Orisha: Eshu   Active

Used in recipes for discharging and spiritual cleansing.

Black nightshade

Sunanum americanum, Sunanum incanum, Sunanum nigrum

Liturgical Names: Ewé Ègùnmò, Odu, Ìgbò

Ruling Orisha: Omolu

Element of Nature: Earth

Magical Classification: Male / Active

It hides intentions; it is excellent for convincing.

Boldo

Plectranthusbrus barbatus

Liturgical Name: Ewé Bàbá

Ruling Orisha: Oshala

Element of Nature: Air

Magical Classification: Female / Passive

Attracts peace and harmony; helps obtain sound advice; balances emotions; helps find help in times of need; brings professional success.

Borage

Other Popular Name: Starflower
Borago officinalis

Ruling Orishas: Iansã, Ogun

Element of Nature: Earth, Fire

Magical Classification: Male / Active

Helps to face difficulties; attracts good energies; strengthens mediumship and spirituality.

Brazilian green propolis

Other Popular Name: Alecrim-do-campo
Baccharis dracunculifolia

Ruling Orisha: Oshala

Element of Nature: Air

Magical Classification: Female / Passive

Spiritual cleansing, against envy and the evil eye.

Brazilian guava

Psidium guineense

Ruling Orisha: Oshossi

Element of Nature: Earth

Magical Classification: Male / Active

Used for spiritual purification and meditation.

Brazilian vervain

Verbena boyanarensis, Verbena canadensis, Verbena hybrida,
Verbena officinalis

Ruling Orishas: Yemaya, Oshala   **Magical Classification:** Female /
Elements of Nature: Air, Water   Passive

Wards off sadness, negativity, and melancholy; attracts love; facilitates concentration and meditation; makes you look capable and pleasant; releases negative energies, bringing creativity, resourcefulness, joy, and good spirits.

Burdock

Aburdockrctium lappa

Ruling Orishas: Eshu, Nana,   **Magical Classification:** Male /
Omolu, Oshumare   Active
Element of Nature: Earth

Used in recipes for discharging and spiritual cleansing.

Burn nettle

Urtica, Urtica dioica

Liturgical Name: Kan-kan   **Magical Classification:** Male /
Ruling Orisha: Eshu   Active
Element of Nature: Fire

Used in recipes for discharging and spiritual cleansing.

Cabreuva

Myrocarpus frondosus

Ruling Orisha: Ogun   **Magical Classification:** Male /
Element of Nature: Earth   Active

Used in recipes for discharging and spiritual cleansing.

Cactus

Euphorbia lateriflora

Liturgical Names: Enu Ekure,   **Ruling Orisha:** Eshu
Enu-òpírè, Igi Oró, Oró, Oró   **Element of Nature:** Fire
Adétè, Oró Elewé, Oró Enu Kò   **Magical Classification:** Male /
Piyè, Oró Wére   Active

All species of cactus are defense plants, removing envy and evil intentions and absorbing negativity.

Calabash tree

Crescentia cujete

Liturgical name: Igbá

Ruling Orishas: Oshala, Oshun

Elements of Nature: Air, Water

Magical Classification: Female / Passive

Its leaves are bound and used to combat evil spells and strengthen beneficial spells.

Calendula

Other Popular Names: Marigold

Calendula officinalis

Liturgical Name: Ewé Pépé

Ruling Orishas: Iansã, Yemaya, Oshun

Element of Nature: Water

Magical Classification: Female / Passive

Flowers are exciting for mood and sexuality; they fight sadness and melancholy and bring protection.

Cambuí-amarelo

Myrciaria delicatula

Ruling Orisha: Iansã

Element of Nature: Water

Magical Classification: Female / Passive

Used in recipes for discharging and spiritual cleansing.

Camellia

Camellia

Ruling Orisha: Oshala

Element of Nature: Air

Magical Classification: Female / Passive

Strengthens and attracts love and passion; it provides plenty and abundance.

Camphor

Cinnamomum camphora, Laurus camphora

Ruling Orishas: Eshu, Oshun

Element of Nature: Water

Magical Classification: Female / Passive

Opens channels for spiritual communication and clairvoyance; eliminates negative energies; strengthens mediumship.

Canafistula palm

Other Popular Name: Chuva-de-ouro
Cassia ferruginea

Liturgical Name: Fitíba
Ruling Orishas: Eshu, Oshun
Element of Nature: Water

Magical Classification: Female/Passive

Opens paths; attracts prosperity, abundance, and plenty; favors fertility and fecundity; strengthens mediumship and spirituality; strengthens and attracts love, passion, and seduction.

Cancharana

Other Popular Names: Canjerana, pau-santo
Cabralea oblongifolia

Ruling Orisha: Ogun
Element of Nature: Earth

Magical Classification: Male/Active

Eliminates evil thoughts and nightmares.

Caper bush

Capparis spinosa

Ruling Orishas: Yemaya, Oshumare
Element of Nature: Water

Magical Classification: Female/Passive

Increases the power of attraction and sensuality; excellent for treating male and female impotence.

Capulin cherry

Prunus salicifolia, Prunus serotina

Liturgical Name: Irú Èso Òyìnbó Kan
Ruling Orisha: Iansã

Element of Nature: Fire
Magical Classification: Female/Passive

Attracts love, seduction, and beauty; acts especially on feminine sensuality and sexuality.

Cará (Brazilian yam)

Other Popular Name: Air potato
Dioscorea alata, Dioscorea bulbifera, Dioscorea dumetorum

Liturgical Names: Akan, Ewura
Esi, Isu Eleso, Isu-èsúrú, Èsúru
Ruling Orishas: Ogun,
Oshoguian

Elements of Nature: Earth
Magical Classification: Male /
Active

Opens paths to success and progress; acts especially on male fertility
and fecundity; its leaves are used in love and union spells.

Caraway

Carum carvi

Ruling Orisha: Oshun
Element of Nature: Water

Magical Classification: Female /
Passive

Increases the power of attraction and sensuality; excellent for treating
female impotence; serves as an amulet against negative influence.

Cardamom

Other Popular Names: True cardamom, green cardamom
Elettaria cardamomum

Ruling Orishas: Yemaya, Ogun
Elements of Nature: Water,
Earth

Magical Classification: Male /
Active

Consolidates desires; excellent in love and sexual spells; strengthens
and attracts love and passion.

Caribbean agave

Agave angustifolia

Ruling Orisha: Omolu
Element of Nature: Earth

Magical Classification: Male /
Active

Cleans the energies of environments and people.

Carica papaya

Carica digitata, Jacaratia digitata, Papaya digitata

Liturgical Names: Síbo, Ìbépé
Ruling Orishas: Eshu
Element of Nature: Fire

Magical Classification: Male /
Active

Used in recipes for discharging and spiritual cleansing.

Carnation
Dianthus caryophyllus
Ruling Orishas: Iansã, Shango   **Magical Classification:** Male /
Element of Nature: Fire   Active

Opens paths; attracts good energies; destroys negative energies; strengthens and attracts love, passion, and seduction in men; strengthens leadership instincts.

Carnauba palm
Copernica prunifera
Ruling Orisha: Oshala   **Magical Classification:** Female /
Element of Nature: Air   Passive

Strengthens the spiritual body and favors connection with the sacred.

Carobinha
Jacaranda brasiliana, Jacaranda decurrens, Jacaranda semiserrata
Ruling Orisha: Omolu   **Magical Classification:** Male /
Element of Nature: Earth   Active

Used in recipes for spiritual discharging.

Carrot
Other Popular Name: Queen Anne's lace
Daucus carota
Liturgical Names: Karoti, Ohun   **Element of Nature:** Earth
Ògbìn Kan   **Magical Classification:** Male /
Ruling Orisha: Oshossi   Active

Consolidates desires; excellent in love spells and sexual spells; strengthens and attracts love and passion.

Cascara sagrada
Other Popular Name: Cascara buckthorn
Rhamnus purshiana
Ruling Orisha: Shango   **Magical Classification:** Male /
Element of Nature: Fire   Active

Relieves trauma and emotional shock; attracts money and protection; fights sadness and melancholy; protects and assists in the solution of justice problems.

Cassia

Cassia sericea

Ruling Orisha: Eshu   **Magical Classification:** Male /
Element of Nature: Fire   Active

Used in recipes for discharging and spiritual cleansing.

Castor bean, purple

Ricinus communis

Liturgical Name: Ewé Lárà Púpà   **Nature elemens:** Fire, Earth
Ruling Orishas: Eshu, Omolu,   **Magical Classification:** Male /
Ossain   Active

Used as a container for offerings related to funeral rituals and the dead,
it has no use in baths and fumigations.

Castor bean, red

Ricinus communis

Liturgical Name: Ewé Lárà   **Elements of Nature:** Fire, Earth
Dundun   **Magical Classification:** Male /
Ruling Orishas: Eshu, Omolu,   Active
Ossain

It represents the holy field and the sacred ground; it is the best choice
to use as a base of support and "towel" on which to lower the ebós and
offerings of Eshu and all the orishas.

Castor bean, sanguineus

Other Popular Name: Mamona
Ricinus sanguineus

Liturgical Name: Ewé Lárà   **Elements of Nature:** Fire, Earth
Ruling Orishas: Eshu, Omolu,   **Magical Classification:** Male /
Ossain   Active

Used as a container for offerings to the deities.

Cathedral bells

Kalanchoe pinnata

Liturgical Names: Eru Ori-   **Element of Nature:** Water
dundun, Àbá Modá   **Magical Classification:** Female /
Ruling Orishas: Eshu, Oshala   Passive

Opens paths; attracts good energies; consolidates desires; strengthens
mediumship and spirituality; strengthens leadership instincts.

Catinga-de-mulata tansy

Other Popular Name: Tansy
Tanacetum vulgare
Liturgical Name: Moborò   **Magical Classification:** Female/
Ruling Orishas: Iansã, Yemaya   Passive
Element of Nature: Water

Helps to react well in the face of hurt and heartbreak; used in recipes for discharging and spiritual cleansing.

Catinguera

Caesalpinia pyramidalis
Ruling Orisha: Eshu   **Magical Classification:** Male/
Element of Nature: Fire   Active

Used in recipes for discharging and spiritual cleansing.

Catnip

Nepeta cataria
Ruling Orisha: Iansã   **Magical Classification:** Male/
Element of Nature: Fire   Active

Consolidates desires; excellent in love and sexual spells; strengthens and attracts love, passion, and beauty.

Catuaba

Trichilia catigua
Liturgical Name: Ajìgbagbó   **Magical Classification:** Male/
Ruling Orishas: Iansã, Shango   Active
Element of Nature: Fire

Consolidates desires; excellent in love spells and sexual spells; strengthens and attracts love and passion.

Celery

Apium graveolens
Ruling Orishas: Omolu, Oshossi   **Magical Classification:** Male/
Element of Nature: Earth   Active

Increases psychic powers; strengthens the spirits and improves mental disposition; brings tranquility to the home.

Cha de bugre

Hedyosmum brasiliense

Ruling Orisha: Oshossi

Element of Nature: Earth

Magical Classification: Male / Active

Attracts and strengthens prosperity and abundance.

Chamomile

Matricaria chamomilla

Ruling Orishas: Oshala, Oshun

Elements of Nature: Air, Water

Magical Classification: Female / Passive

Attracts money and prosperity; strengthens brotherly love; provides peaceful dreams; purifies the soul; and calms the heart.

Chaptalia

Other Popular Names: Silverpuff
Chaptalia nutans

Liturgical Names: Jimi, Òpásóró

Ruling Orishas: Eshu, Yemaya, Oshumare, Shango

Elements of Nature: Water, Fire

Magical Classification: Male / Active

Brings out the liar and the gossip; it reveals secrets.

Charcoal tree

Other Popular Names: Indian charcoal tree, gunpowder tree, pigeonwood, motambo
Trema orientalis

Liturgical Name: Afére

Ruling Orisha: Iyewa

Element of Nature: Water

Magical Classification: Female / Passive

It is considered the protective tree of friendship, and its leaves are capable of putting an end to discord and disunity. Care must be taken to harvest only the necessary amount of leaves; otherwise, it has the opposite effect.

Chestnut

Other Popular Name: Brazil nut
Bertholletia excelsa

Liturgical Name: Igi Ósè

Ruling Orishas: Oshun, Shango

Elements of Nature: Fire, Water

Magical Classification: Female / Passive

Attracts wisdom, money, and good luck; favors fertility and the home's maintenance and protection; brings strength, security, and courage to the paths.

Chinaberry

Other Popular Name: Persian lilac
Melia azedarach

Liturgical Names: Afóforo Ìgbàlódé, Afóforo Òyínbó, Eké Ilè, Eké Òyínbó, Ekéòyìnbó, Ewé Mesán, Igi Mesán

Ruling Orishas: Iansã, Shango
Element of Nature: Fire
Magical Classification: Male/ Active

Cancels spells and negative energies; destroys negative fluids and the influence of evil spirits; brings strength and courage to face challenges.

Chinese lantern

Other Popular Name: Painted Abutilon
Abutilon pictum, Abutilon striatum, Abutilon venosum

Ruling Orisha: Eshu
Element of Nature: Fire
Magical Classification: Male/ Active

Used in recipes for discharging and spiritual cleansing.

Cider grass

Andropogon citratus

Ruling Orishas: Ogun, Oshala
Element of Nature: Air
Magical Classification: Female/ Passive

Helps to react well in the face of hurt and heartbreak; it assists in the treatment for insomnia and anxiety.

Cinnamon

Cinnamomum zeylanicum

Liturgical Name: Ojugun
Ruling Orisha: Iansã
Element of Nature: Fire
Magical Classification: Female/ Passive

Opens the path to professional success; attracts love and balances emotions; attracts prosperity; favors business and acquisition and material goods.

Cinquefoil

Potentilla glandulosa, Potentilla reptans

Ruling Orisha: Oshala   **Magical Classification:** Female/
Element of Nature: Air   Passive

Used in recipes for discharging and spiritual cleansing.

Cipó-caboclo

Davilla rugosa

Ruling Orisha: Oshossi   **Magical Classification:** Male/
Element of Nature: Earth   Active

Used in recipes for spiritual discharging.

Cipó-camarão ("Shrimp vine")

Bignonia eximia

Ruling Orisha: Oshossi   **Magical Classification:** Male/
Element of Nature: Earth   Active

Used in recipes for discharging and spiritual cleansing.

Climbing dayflower

Other Popular Name: Tropical spiderwort
Commelina diffusa l.

Liturgical Name: Gòdògbódò   **Magical Classification:** Female/
Ruling Orishas: Yemaya, Oshun   Passive
Element of Nature: Water

Sharpens intelligence; reduces mental confusion and indecision; provides recognition; stimulates love and seduction; strengthens mediumship and spirituality.

Clove

Eugenia caryophyllata, Syzygium aromaticum

Liturgical Name: Irú Òdòdó Kan   **Magical Classification:** Male/
Ruling Orisha: Iansã   Active
Element of Nature: Fire

Attracts money and prosperity; favors love and sex; protects from malicious people and negative thoughts; puts an end to gossip and whispering. It is one of the most potent fumigations to protect against spirits and evil spirits.

Cobblers peg

Other Popular Name: Black-jack, beggarticks, picão-da-praia
Bidens pilosa

Liturgical Name: Abéré Olòko
Ruling Orishas: Eshu, Omolu
Elements of Nature: Earth, Fire

Magical Classification: Male /
Active

Used in recipes for discharging and spiritual cleansing.

Cockspur coral

Erythrina crista-galli

Ruling Orisha: Yemaya
Element of Nature: Water

Magical Classification: Female /
Passive

Used in recipes for discharging and spiritual cleansing.

Coconut

Cocos nucifera

Liturgical Name: Àgbon
Ruling Orishas: Oshala, Oshossi
Elements of Nature: Air, Earth

Magical Classification: Male /
Active

Encourages contact with spirituality; brings the emotional balance necessary for decision making.

Coffee

Coffea arabica

Liturgical Names: Kofi, Owó Ide
Ruling Orisha: Omolu
Element of Nature: Earth

Magical Classification: Male /
Active

Eliminates evil thoughts and nightmares; excellent against harmful spirits.

Coffee senna

Other Popular Names: Stinking goosefoot, antbush,
coffeeweed, septicweed
Cassia occidentalis

Liturgical Name: Ewé Réré
Ruling Orisha: Eshu
Element of Nature: Fire

Magical Classification: Male /
Active

Its branches are used in defense rituals; it is very useful for cleaning the place where Eshu's points were scratched and areas where his offerings were burned.

Colônia

Renealmia brasiliensis

Liturgical Name: Tótó

Ruling Orishas: Iyewa, Yemaya, Oshala

Elements of Nature: Air, Water

Magical Classification: Female/ Passive

Draws good energies in all areas of life; harmonizes the physical body and spiritual body; attracts.

Comfrey

Symphytum officinale

Ruling Orisha: Oshala

Element of Nature: Air

Magical Classification: Female/ Passive

Makes others comfortable when they are in the presence of those who use it; gives serenity to behavior and words; strengthens self-confidence in interviews and meetings.

Common juniper

Juniperus communis

Ruling Orishas: Iansã, Ogun

Element of Nature: Earth

Magical Classification: Male/ Active

Keeps away the evil eye and envy; strengthens and attracts love, passion, and seduction; brings strength, courage, peace, and divine protection.

Coral plant

Jatropha multifida

Liturgical Name: Bòtújè

Ruling Orisha: Eshu

Element of Nature: Fire

Magical Classification: Male/ Active

Used in recipes for discharging and spiritual cleansing.

Coral vine

Other Popular Name: Mexican creeper

Antigonon leptopus

Ruling Orishas: Oshun, Shango

Elements of Nature: Fire, Water

Magical Classification: Female/ Passive

Consolidates desires; excellent in love spells and sexual spells; strengthens and attracts love, passion, and seduction.

Coriander

Coriandrum sativum

Ruling Orisha: Oshun **Magical Classification:** Female/
Element of Nature: Water Passive

Consolidates desires and strengthens; attracts love, passion, and seduction; brings brightness, success, and recognition.

Corn

Other Popular Name: Maize
Zea mays

Liturgical Names: Egbáado, Okà, **Element of Nature:** Earth
Yángán, Àgbàdo, Àgbàdo Pupa, **Magical Classification:** Male/
Ìgbàdo, Óoká Active
Ruling Orishas: Logunede,
Oshossi

Opens paths; attracts prosperity, abundance, and plenty; favors fertility and fecundity; strengthens mediumship and spirituality; strengthens and attracts love.

Corn plant

Other Popular Name: Nativo
Dracena fragrans

Liturgical Name: Pèrégún **Element of Nature:** Fire
Ruling Orishas: Iansã, Obba, **Magical Classification:** Male/
Ogun Active

Opens the path to good luck and the pursuit of excellence, progress, and courage; relieves the burden of those who suffer humiliation.

Corn silk

Zea mays

Liturgical Name: Efon **Magical Classification:** Male/
Ruling Orisha: Oshossi Active
Element of Nature: Earth

It provides plenty and abundance; it is an excellent complement to the prosperity powders.

Crack-open

Casearia sylvestris

Liturgical Name: Alékèsì

Ruling Orishas: Ogun, Oshossi

Elements of Nature: Earth, Fire

Magical Classification: Male /
Active

Opens paths; attracts prosperity, abundance, and plenty; attracts good energies; strengthens leadership.

Creeping charlie

Pilea nummulariifolia

Ruling Orishas: Oshun, Oshossi

Elements of Nature: Earth, Water

Magical Classification: Male /
Active

Opens paths and attracts prosperity, abundance, and plentifulness; attracts good energies; strengthens leadership instincts.

Cumana

Other Popular Names: Cipó-de-cumanã, cunanã

Euphorbia phosphorea

Ruling Orisha: Eshu

Element of Nature: Fire

Magical Classification: Male /
Active

Used in recipes for spiritual discharging and cleansing.

Cumin

Cuminum cyminum

Ruling Orishas: Oshun, Shango

Element of Nature: Fire

Magical Classification: Male /
Active

Stimulates love, truth, loyalty, and fidelity.

Cypress

Chamaecyparis, Cupressus

Liturgical Name: Igi Ikú

Ruling Orisha: Nana

Element of Nature: Water

Magical Classification: Female /
Passive

Increases concentration and firmness of thoughts; brings longevity, health, and emotional balance.

Daffodil

Narcissus cyclamineus

Ruling Orishas: Ossain, Oshala
Elements of Nature: Earth, Air

Magical Classification: Female /
Passive

Attracts harmony, peace, and quiet thoughts; excellent in the body and environment's spiritual purification; strengthens friendships and social relations.

Devil nettle

Other Popular Name: Spurge nettle
Jatropha urens

Ruling Orisha: Omolu
Element of Nature: Fire

Magical Classification: Male /
Active

Used in recipes for discharging and spiritual cleansing.

Devil's-pepper

Rauwolfia vomitoria

Liturgical Names: Aso Feyeje,
Ewé Òóra
Ruling Orisha: Oshossi

Element of Nature: Earth
Magical Classification: Male /
Active

Opens paths; attracts prosperity, abundance, and plentifulness; attracts good energies; strengthens leadership instincts.

Dill

Anethum graveolens

Ruling Orishas: Oshun, Oshossi
Elements of Nature: Earth,
Water

Magical Classification: Male /
Active

Fights sadness and melancholy; helps attract money and favors; and brings love and protection to the home.

Dragon's blood

Croton lechleri

Ruling Orisha: Ogun
Element of Nature: Fire

Magical Classification: Male /
Active

Opens paths; attracts good energies; consolidatess desires; strengthens mediumship and spirituality; strengthens leadership instincts.

Dragon-tail plant

Epipremnum pinnatum

Liturgical Name: Ewé Dan
Ruling Orishas: Iyewa, Oshumare, Shango

Elements of Nature: Earth, Fire
Magical Classification: Male/Active

Protects against betrayals and lies of all kinds.

Dumb cane

Dieffenbachia exotica alba, Dieffenbachia seguine

Liturgical Names: Wobomú, Wobomú Funfun
Ruling Orishas: Eshu, Ogun

Elements of Nature: Earth, Fire
Magical Classification: Male/Active

Used in recipes for spiritual discharging.

Dutch eggplant

Other Popular Names: Joah, love-apple
Sunanum aculeatissimum

Liturgical Name: Ewé Bòbó
Ruling Orishas: Eshu, Ogun, Omolu

Element of Nature: Earth
Magical Classification: Male/Active

Its fruit is used in removal powders, but it should never be consumed because it is highly poisonous.

Dutchman's pipe

Aristolochia esperanzae, Aristolochia sylvicola,
Aristolochia triangularis

Liturgical Names: Jokónijé, Jókójé
Ruling Orishas: Oshumare, Shango

Elements of Nature: Earth, Fire
Magical Classification: Male/Active

Consolidates desires; excellent in love spells and sexual spells; strengthens and attracts love, passion, and seduction.

Elderberry

Other Popular Names: Elder, black elder, European elder
Sambucus nigra

Liturgical Name: Àtòrìnà
Ruling Orisha: Omolu
Element of Nature: Earth

Magical Classification: Male/Active

Cancels spells and negative energies; brings strength and courage.

Elephant's foot

Other Popular Name: Tobacco weed
Elephantopus mollis, Sunanum mauritianum

Liturgical Names: Arójòkú, Ode Ákosùn
Ruling Orisha: Shango
Element of Nature: Fire
Magical Classification: Male / Active

Used in recipes for discharging and spiritual cleansing.

Elm

Ulmus minor

Ruling Orisha: Iansã
Element of Nature: Fire
Magical Classification: Male / Active

Consolidates desires; strengthens and attracts love, passion, and seduction; strengthens the spiritual body.

Erva-preá

Other Popular Names: Rokshan, wild patchouli
Cyrtocymura scorpioides

Ruling Orisha: Eshu
Element of Nature: Fire
Magical Classification: Male / Active

Used in recipes for discharging and spiritual cleansing.

Erva-tostão ("Penny-weed")

Boerhavia hirsuta

Liturgical Name: Étìpónlá
Ruling Orisha: Ogun
Element of Nature: Earth
Magical Classification: Male / Active

Prevents poverty; helps find new jobs and professional opportunities; keeps negative energies away.

Ethiopian pepper

Xylopia aethiopica

Liturgical Name: Ataare
Ruling Orisha: Eshu
Element of Nature: Fire
Magical Classification: Male / Active

Attracts good luck; eliminates fights at home and work.

Eucalyptus

Eucalyptus
Ruling Orisha: Oshala
Element of Nature: Air
Magical Classification: Female /
Passive

Cleansing, energizing, and spiritual protection.

Facheiro

Cereus squamosus, Facheiroa publiflora, Zehntnerella squamulosa
Ruling Orisha: Eshu
Element of Nature: Fire
Magical Classification: Male /
Active

Used in recipes for discharging and spiritual cleansing.

Fennel

Ocimum guineensis
Liturgical Name: Efinrín
Èrùyánntefé
Ruling Orishas: Oshala, Oshun
Element of Nature: Air
Magical Classification: Female /
Passive

Helps against insomnia and anxiety; effective against "big eye," or to have your eye on something; improves the ability to speak in public and make speeches; personal protection; brings harmony and calm.

Flor-do-campo ("Wildflowers")

Gaya macrantha
Ruling Orishas: Iyewa, Iansã,
Oshun
Element of Nature: Water
Magical Classification: Female /
Passive

Attracts prosperity, abundance, and love.

Florida burrhead

Other Popular Name: Chá-verde
Echinodorus grandiflorus
Liturgical Name: Ewé Séséré
Ruing Orishas: Omolu, Oshossi
Element of Nature: Earth
Magical Classification: Male /
Active

Helps overcome relationship breakdowns; combats loneliness and sadness; harmonizes couples.

Flower of souls

Other Popular Names: Maria-mole, flor-das-almas
Senecio brasiliensis

Ruling Orisha: Eshu
Element of Nature: Fire

Magical Classification: Male /
Active

Used in recipes for discharging and spiritual cleansing.

Four o' clock flower

Other Popular Name: Marvel of Peru
Mirabilis jalapa

Liturgical Name: Èkelèyi
Ruling Orishas: Iyewa, Iansã,
Oshun

Element of Nature: Water
Magical Classification: Female /
Passive

Sharpens intelligence; reduces mental confusion and indecision; gives radiance and recognition; stimulates love and seduction; strengthens mediumship and spirituality.

Frangipani

Plumeria

Ruling Orisha: Omolu
Element of Nature: Earth

Magical Classification: Male /
Active

Keeps away negative spirits and influences from the dead; is excellent in spiritual cleansing and purification.

Frankincense

Boswella carterii

Ruling Orisha: Oshun
Element of Nature: Water

Magical Classification: Female /
Passive

Opens paths; attracts good energies; favors contact with the sacred; strengthens mediumship and spirituality.

Fuchsia

Fuchsia hybrida, Fuchsia magellania, Fuchsia regia

Ruling Orisha: Eshu
Element of Nature: Fire

Magical Classification: Male /
Active

Used in recipes for spiritual discharging.

Fumitory

Fumaria officinalis

Ruling Orishas: Omolu, Ossain, Oshossi

Magical Classification: Male / Active

Element of Nature: Earth

Linked to the powers of wealth and prosperity; passed around the house and on the soles of the shoes like a spray to attract money.

Gale-of-the-wind

Other Popular Names: Stone breaker, pick-a-back, quebra-demanda
Phyllanthus amarus, Phyllanthus fraternus, Phyllanthus muellerianus

Liturgical Names: Arunjeran, Dobísowo, Ewé Bojútóna, Ewé Bíyemí, Eyín Olobe, Èhìn Olobe

Elements of Nature: Earth, Fire

Magical Classification: Male / Active

Ruling Orishas: Ogun, Shango

Helps overcome relationship breakdowns; brings strength and courage to face challenges.

Garlic

Allium sativum

Liturgical Name: Aáyù

Ruling Orishas: Eshu, Omolu

Elements of Nature: Earth, Fire

Magical Classification: Male / Active

Wards off bad vibrations and evil spirits; used to eliminate negative forms of obsessive thoughts.

Garlic plant

Other Popular Name: Pau-d'alho
Gallesia integrifolia

Ruling Orisha: Eshu

Element of Nature: Fire

Magical Classification: Male / Active

Baths are performed at crossroads, in which, after the bath, an offering of *farofa de dendê* (farinha or manioc flour combined with red palm oil) should immediately be made to Eshu; used in recipes for discharging and spiritual cleaning.

Garlic skin
Allium sativum
Liturgical Name: Aáyù
Ruling Orishas: Eshu, Ossain
Element of Nature: Fire
Magical Classification: Male /
Active

Removes the dangers of theft and robbery; exorcises harmful spirits and energies; spiritual and physical protection and defense.

Genipap
Genipa americana
Liturgical Name: Bujè
Ruling Orishas: Eshu, Iansã, Omolu
Elements of Nature: Earth, Fire
Magical Classification: Male /
Active

Used in recipes for discharging and spiritual cleansing.

Geranium
Pelargonium, Pelargonium odoratissimum
Liturgical Name: Ewé Púpayo
Ruling Orishas: Eshu, Shango
Element of Nature: Fire
Magical Classification: Male /
Active

Relieves tension, nervousness, and anxiety, soothing and harmonizing personal thoughts and energies; brings strength and vitality to the body and soul.

Ginger
Zingiber officinale
Liturgical Name: Atale
Ruling Orishas: Iansã, Shango, Oshun
Element of Nature: Fire
Magical Classification: Male /
Active

Opens paths; attracts prosperity, abundance, and plenty; attracts good energies; strengthens leadership.

Ginseng
Panax gingseng
Ruling Orishas: Oshun, Shango
Element of Nature: Fire
Magical Classification: Male /
Active

Facilitates learning and improves the ability to learn; fulfills wishes; strengthens and attracts love.

Globe amaranth

Gomphrena globosa
Liturgical Name: Èkèlegbàrá   **Magical Classification:** Male /
Ruling Orisha: Eshu   Active
Element of Nature: Fire

Used for spiritual cleansing and discharging.

Gold button

Other Popular Name: Botão-de-ouro
Cyathula prostrata
Liturgical Name: Àwúrepépé   **Magical Classification:** Female /
Ruling Orisha: Oshun   Passive
Element of Nature: Water

Attracts prosperity, abundance, and plenty; stimulates and strengthens compassion; facilitates obtaining favors and advantages; brings joy and happiness.

Grains of paradise

Other Popular Name: Guinea pepper
Aframomum melegueta
Liturgical Names: Erinje, Erunje,   **Element of Nature:** Fire
Igi Àta, Olorin, Sésédo, Àtàré,   **Magical Classification:** Male /
Èrù, Ééru Àwónká   Active
Ruling Orisha: Eshu

Warms the paths and gives movement to desires; prevents and wards off pain and tears for losses; transmutes the negative into positive; brings joy and achievements; brings knowledge and enlightenment; is an activating and multiplying principle of spells.

Grape

Vitis
Liturgical Name: Èso Àjàrà   **Magical Classification:** Female /
Ruling Orishas: Iansã, Oshun   Passive
Element of Nature: Water

Attracts prosperity, abundance, and plenty; favors fertility and fecundity; strengthens and attracts love.

Greater celandine

Chelidonium majus
Ruling Orishas: Omolu, Ossain   **Magical Classification:** Male /
Element of Nature: Earth   Active

Used in recipes for discharging and spiritual cleansing.

Guaco

Mikania glomerata
Liturgical Name: Ójé Dúdú   **Magical Classification:** Male /
Ruling Orishas: Oshala, Oshossi Active
Elements of Nature: Air, Earth

Relieves feelings of loneliness and abandonment; strengthens friendships and social behavior.

Guadua bamboo

Other Popular Names: Timber bamboo
Guadua angustifolia
Ruling Orisha: Shango   **Magical Classification:** Male /
Element of Nature: Fire   Active

Used in recipes for discharging and spiritual cleansing.

Guararema

Gallesia gorazema
Ruling Orisha: Omolu   **Magical Classification:** Male /
Element of Nature: Earth   Active

Used for the purification and breaking of curses.

Guinea hen weed

Petiveria alliaceae
Liturgical Name: Ojusaju   **Magical Classification:** Male /
Ruling Orishas: Ossain, Oshossi Active
Element of Nature: Earth

Used in recipes for spiritual discharging.

Hog plum

Other Popular Names: Caja, yellow mombin, African grape
Pseudospondias microcarpa, Spondias mombin

Liturgical Names: Ekikà, Iléwo
Olósán, Olósán, Ìyeyè

Element of Nature: Earth

Magical Classification: Male /
Active

Ruling Orishas: Ogun, Ossain

Protects against physical, energetic, and spiritual theft and attacks by malicious and stupid people.

Holly

Quercus iles, Quercus rotindifolia

Ruling Orisha: Eshu

Magical Classification: Male /
Active

Element of Nature: Fire

Used in various forms of magic as a way to seal spiritual covenants and commitments.

Honey spurge

Euphorbia mellifera

Liturgical Name: Àgogo

Magical Classification: Male /
Active

Ruling Orisha: Eshu

Element of Nature: Fire

Combined with other ingredients, it seals pacts and spiritual commitments; widely used in magic seals and scratched points; and concentration point for the forces of the *eshus* (spirits) of Kimbanda.

Honeysuckle

Lonicera periclymenum

Ruling Orishas: Iansã, Iyewa,
Oshun

Magical Classification: Female /
Passive

Element of Nature: Water

Favors intuition, creativity, and prosperity.

Horsetail

Other Popular Name: Cavalinha
Equisetum arvense, Equisetum bogotense

Ruling Orishas: Oshumare,
Shango

Magical Classification: Male /
Active

Elements of Nature: Fire, Earth

Protects women and blesses the womb, bringing fertility.

Horsewood

Clausena anisata

Liturgical Names: Agbásá, Àtàpàrí Òbúko

Ruling Orisha: Iansã

Element of Nature: Fire

Magical Classification: Female / Passive

Used in recipes for discharge and spiritual cleansing.

Indigo

Other Popular Names: Bengal indigo, Java indigo, Natal indigo
Indigofera arrecta, Indigofera suffruticosa, Indigofera tinctoria

Liturgical Names: Elú-weere, Elú-àjà

Ruling Orisha: Oshala

Element of Nature: Air

Magical Classification: Female / Passive

Excellent for spiritual cleansing and purification.

Iri palm

Other Popular Name: Brejauva palm
Astrocaryum aculeatissimum, Astrocaryum ayri, Toxophoenix aculeatissima

Ruling Orishas: Yemaya, Oshossi

Elements of Nature: Earth, Water

Magical Classification: Male / Active

Used in recipes for discharging and spiritual cleansing.

Iroko

Other Popular Name: African teak
Chlorophora excelsa, Ficus doliaria

Liturgical Name: Ìrókò

Ruling Orishas: Irôco, Oshala

Element of Nature: Air

Magical Classification: Female / Passive

It is home to both male and female ancestors, considered one of the trees of the world's creation. Its strength of spiritual fixation is so great that it must be used with great care, because it can, when mishandled, fix behaviors.

Ivy

Hedera helix

Liturgical Name: Ìtakùn Ewéko   **Elements of Nature:** Earth,
Ruling Orishas: Oshumare,   Water
Oshossi   **Magical Classification:** Male /
   Active

Attracts happiness and personal and professional recognition.

Jabuticaba

Other Popular Name: Brazilian grape tree
Plinia cauliflora

Ruling Orishas: Ogun, Omolu   **Magical Classification:** Male /
Element of Nature: Earth   Active

Used in recipes for discharge and spiritual cleansing.

Jackfruit

Artcarpus heterophyllu, Artocarpus integrifolia

Liturgical Name: Topónúrìn   **Magical Classification:** Male /
Ruling Orisha: Oshossi   Active
Element of Nature: Earth

Specific spells with jackfruit transform the brute man into a noble, valuable, and enlightened being; it is the home of the great ancestral mothers, to whom we implore long life, without tribulations or punishment.

Jasmine

Jasminum

Liturgical Name: Ògàn Fúnfún   **Magical Classification:** Female /
Ruling Orisha: Oshala   Passive
Element of Nature: Air

Helps avoid quarrels and misunderstandings, calms the environment, improves mood, and improves business.

Jequirity bean

Other Popular Name: Rosary pea
Abrus precatorius

Liturgical Name: Owérénjéjé

Magical Classification: Male /
Active

Ruling Orishas: Eshu, Oshala

Element of Nature: Fire

The leaves end fights, strengthen the union between members of a group, bring peace and harmony, and win struggles without violence. The seed causes the opposite effect.

Job's tears

Other Popular Name: Adlay millet
Coix lacryma-jobi

Liturgical Name: Ewé Oju Omi

Magical Classification: Female /
Passive

Ruling Orishas: Yemaya, Ossain

Elements of Nature: Earth,
Water

The leaves and seeds are recommended for bathing the eyes early in the morning, providing well-being and physical and emotional balance—the night before, the preparation should be left out in the open, in calm weather, and be removed before sunrise.

Johnny jump-up

Viola tricolor

Ruling Orisha: Oshun

Magical Classification: Female /
Passive

Element of Nature: Water

Eliminates negative charges; brings love and purification.

Jungle plum

Sideroxylon obtusifolium

Ruling Orisha: Eshu

Magical Classification: Male /
Active

Element of Nature: Fire

Used in recipes for discharging and spiritual cleansing.

Jurema-branca

Piptadenia stipulacea

Ruling Orisha: Oshossi

Magical Classification: Male /
Active

Element of Nature: Earth

Opens paths; attracts good energies; strengthens mediumship and spirituality; brings strength and courage to face challenges.

Jurema-preta

Acacia jurema, Mimosa tenuiflora

Liturgical Name: Èwòn Dundun
Ruling Orisha: Eshu
Element of Nature: Fire

Magical Classification: Male / Active

Opens paths; attracts good energies; strengthens mediumship and spirituality; brings strength and courage to face challenges; used in strong discharge baths.

Jurubeba

Sunanum paniculatum

Liturgical Names: Igba Ajá, Igba Igún
Ruling Orishas: Eshu, Omolu

Element of Nature: Earth
Magical Classification: Male / Active

Opens paths; attracts good energies; strengthens mediumship and spirituality; brings strength and courage to face challenges.

Kalanchoe

Other Popular Names: Saião, folha-da-costa
Kalanchoe brasiliensis

Liturgical Name: Òdúndún
Ruling Orisha: Oshala
Element of Nature: Air

Magical Classification: Female / Passive

Balances the head and thoughts, avoiding anxiety, melancholy, and anguish; brings good thoughts, peace, and tranquility.

Kola nut

Cola acuminata, Cola nitida

Liturgical Names: Igi Obì, Obì
Ruling Orisha: Oshala
Element of Nature: Air

Magical Classification: Female / Passive

It is a substantial offering, present in absolutely all the rituals of Candomblé, and considered an Orisha. Following the correct ritual, it acts as an oracle capable of seeing the past, present, and future.

Lady's thumb

Other Popular Names: Jesusplant, redshank
Polygonum persicaria
Liturgical Name: Eró Igbin
Ruling Orisha: Eshu
Element of Nature: Fire

Magical Classification: Male /
Active

Opens paths; gives serenity to behavior and words; excellent in destroying negative influences; strengthens self-confidence in interviews, meetings, and hearings.

Lantana

Other Popular Name: Shrub verbena
Lantana camara
Liturgical Name: Ábitólá
Ruling Orisha: Oshun
Element of Nature: Water

Magical Classification: Female /
Passive

Used in recipes for discharging and spiritual cleansing.

Lavender

Lavandula angustifolia
Ruling Orisha: Oshala
Element of Nature: Air

Magical Classification: Female /
Passive

Calms down moods, ends fights, eliminates melancholy, and makes you have a peaceful sleep; balances emotions.

Lead vine

Other Popular Name: Chilean dodder
Cuscuta racemosa
Liturgical Name: Awo Pupa
Ruling Orishas: Eshu, Omolu,
Oshun

Elements of Nature: Earth,
Water
Magical Classification: Male /
Active

Used in recipes for discharging and spiritual cleansing.

Lemon

Citrus limon
Liturgical Names: Osán Wewe,
Òrómbo, Òrómbo Wewe
Ruling Orisha: Eshu

Element of Nature: Fire
Magical Classification: Male /
Active

Makes wishes come true; strengthens love and passion.

Lemon balm

Melissa officinalis

Liturgical Name: Ewé Túni
Ruling Orisha: Oshun
Element of Nature: Water

Magical Classification: Female/
Passive

Attracts money and prosperity; favors brotherly love; favors quiet dreams; purifies the soul and calms the heart.

Lemongrass

Cymbopogon citratus

Liturgical Names: Koríko Oba,
Koríko Òyinbó, Koóko Oba
Ruling Orisha: Oshossi

Element of Nature: Earth
Magical Classification: Male/
Active

Encourages the approach of protective spirits.

Lemon-scented gum

Other Popular Name: Lemon eucalyptus
Corymbia citriodora

Ruling Orishas: Iansã, Shango
Element of Nature: Fire

Magical Classification: Male/
Active

Used in recipes for discharging and spiritual cleansing.

Lettuce

Lactuca sativa

Liturgical Names: Irú Èfó Kan,
Yánrin-oko
Ruling Orisha: Iansã

Element of Nature: Water
Magical Classification: Female/
Passive

Opens the channels of spiritual communication and clairvoyance; eliminates negative energies.

Licorice

Glycyrrhiza glabra

Ruling Orisha: Oshala
Element of Nature: Air

Magical Classification: Female/
Passive

Increases the ability to speak in public and give speeches; facilitates learning and the ability to learn.

Licorice weed

Scoparea dulcis

Liturgical Name: Semim-semim
Ruling Orisha: Oshun
Elements of Nature: Water, Fire

Magical Classification: Female/Passive

A powder is made from its roots to make others accept and comply with whatever is said. Excellent for bringing conviction and persuasion.

Lily of the valley

Convallaria majalis

Liturgical Name: Balabá
Ruling Orishas: Oshala, Iansã
Element of Nature: Air

Magical Classification: Female/Passive

Attracts harmony, peace, and peaceful thoughts; excellent in the spiritual purification of the body and surroundings; strengthens friendships and social relationships.

Limão-bravo

Siparuna apiosyce

Liturgical Name: Òrombó Kíkan
Ruling Orisha: Ogun
Element of Nature: Fire

Magical Classification: Male/Active

Used in recipes for discharging and spiritual cleansing.

Littleleaf linden

Tilia cordata, Tilia platyphyllos

Ruling Orisha: Oshala
Element of Nature: Air

Magical Classification: Female/Passive

Gives behavior and words serenity, strengthens self-confidence, projects personal and professional stability.

Loofah

Other Popular Name: Chinese okra
Luffa acutangala

Liturgical Name: Ewé Orira
Ruling Orisha: Omolu
Element of Nature: Earth

Magical Classification: Male/Active

It replaces the bath sponge in magical rituals.

Lotus

Nelumbo nucifera
Liturgical Name: Òsíbàtà
Ruling Orisha: Oshun
Element of Nature: Water

Magical Classification: Female / Passive

Attracts harmony, peace, and quiet thoughts; excellent for bringing brightness and prosperity; favors love, enchantment, and persuasion; widely used for meditation.

Maçã-de-cobra tansy

Other Popular Name: Tansy
Tanacetum vulgaris
Ruling Orishas: Yemaya, Oshala, Oshun
Element of Nature: Water

Magical Classification: Female / Passive

Attracts harmony, peace, and peaceful thoughts; attracts prosperity and happiness; excellent in the spiritual purification of the body and surroundings; strengthens friendships and social relationships; strengthens and attracts love and passion.

Madagascar dragon tree

Dracaena marginata
Ruling Orishas: Eshu, Ogun
Element of Nature: Earth

Magical Classification: Male / Active

Protects against envy; brings growth and progress.

Mãe-boa

Other Popular Name: Cissampelos
Cissampelos fasciculata
Ruling Orishas: Iansã, Yemaya, Oshun
Element of Nature: Water

Magical Classification: Female / Passive

Opens paths; helps to react well in the face of hurt and heartbreak; brings strength and courage to face challenges.

Magnolia

Magnolia grandiflora
Ruling Orishas: Iansã, Iyewa, Oshun
Element of Nature: Water

Magical Classification: Female / Passive

Excellent in sexual magic; favors fertility and fecundity; strengthens mediumship and spirituality; strengthens and attracts love, passion, and seduction.

Maidenhair fern

Adiantum capillus-veneris

Liturgical Name: Ewé Mìmò

Ruling Orishas: Yemaya, Logunede, Oshun

Element of Nature: Water

Magical Classification: Female / Passive

Opens channels of spiritual communication and clairvoyance; attracts love and beauty; favors sympathy and recognition.

Malay apple

Syzygium malaccense

Liturgical Name: Igi Eso Pupa

Ruling Orisha: Ogun

Element of Nature: Earth

Magical Classification: Male / Active

Opens paths; helps to react well to sorrow and disgust; brings strength and courage to face challenges.

Manacá

Other Popular Name: Lady of the night

Brunfelsia uniflora

Ruling Orishas: Nana, Omolu

Elements of Nature: Water, Earth

Magical Classification: Male / Active

Consolidates desires; excellent in love spells and sexual spells; strengthens and attracts love and passion and seduction.

Mango

Mangifera indica

Liturgical Name: Sèrí

Ruling Orishas: Eshu, Ogun

Element of Nature: Earth

Magical Classification: Male / Active

Used in recipes for discharging and spiritual cleansing.

Mangrove

Rhizophora mangle

Ruling Orisha: Omolu

Element of Nature: Earth

Magical Classification: Male / Active

Used in recipes for discharging and spiritual cleansing.

Marigold pepper

Other Popular Name: Pariparoba

Piper marginatum, Pothomorphe umbellata

Liturgical Name: Ewé Ìyá

Ruling Orisha: Yemaya

Element of Nature: Water

Magical Classification: Female / Passive

Avoids melancholy and anguish; it represents the heart of Yemaya, which guides men's heads.

Marjoram

Majorana hortensis, Origanum majorana

Ruling Orishas: Yemaya, Obba, Oshala, Shango

Elements of Nature: Air, Fire

Magical Classification: Female / Passive

Corrective of sexual excesses and lust.

Marsh sugar apple

Other Popular Name: Cabeça-de-nego ("blackhead")

Annona coriacea

Ruling Orisha: Eshu

Element of Nature: Fire

Magical Classification: Male / Active

Used in recipes for discharging and spiritual cleansing.

Melon

Cucumis melo

Liturgical Names: Agbéye, Ègúsí, Ègúsí Agbè, Èso Ìtàkùn

Ruling Orishas: Yemaya, Oshun

Element of Nature: Water

Magical Classification: Female / Passive

Opened as a cup, it is used as a container for spells of union, harmonization, and fertility. Symbolically, it represents the head and the womb, the ability to think and reproduce; its seeds attract love.

Mexican prickly poppy

Other Popular Name: Flowering thistle
Argemone mexicana

Liturgical Names: Akunakun, Egun-arígbó
Ruling Orisha: Eshu

Element of Nature: Fire
Magic Classification: Male / Active

Brings back what was lost.

Mexican tea

Other Popular Names: Jesuit's tea, epazote
Chenopodium ambrosioides

Liturgical Names: Ewé Imí, Manturusí
Ruling Orisha: Eshu

Element of Nature: Fire
Magical Classification: Male / Active

Excellent for spiritual discharge—people who use it should not touch it without covering their hands with cloth or paper and then should discard it at a crossroads.

Mint

Mentha

Ruling Orisha: Oshala
Element of Nature: Air

Magical Classification: Female / Passive

Recommended to lower anxiety, but if used too much, it can alter sleep rhythm; improves attention.

Morning Glory

Other Popular Name: Blue-bell
Ipomoea nil

Liturgical Name: Ejirin Òdàn
Ruling Orisha: Oshossi
Elements of Nature: Earth, Air

Magical Classification: Female / Passive

Opens paths; attracts prosperity, abundance, and fullness; attracts good energies; strengthens leadership.

Moses-in-the-cradle

Other Popular Names: Boat lily, oyster plant
Rhoeo discolor

Liturgical Name: Òbé Sèmi Oya
Ruling Orishas: Iansã, Ogun, Oshossi

Element of Nature: Fire
Magical Classification: Male / Active

Frees the person from people's tongues and gossip; optimum spiritual protection against negative environmental energies.

Moss

Bryophyta

Ruling Orisha: Omolu
Element of Nature: Earth

Magical Classification: Male / Active

Attracts harmony, peace, and quiet thoughts; excels in the spiritual purification of the body and environment; strengthens friendships and social relationships.

Mugwort

Artemisia vulgaris

Ruling Orisha: Shango
Element of Nature: Fire

Magical Classification: Male / Active

Opens channels of spiritual communication and clairvoyance.

Mulberry

Morus nigra

Liturgical Name: Éyà Àgbáyun Dúdú Kan
Ruling Orisha: Eshu

Element of Nature: Fire
Magical Classification: Male / Active

Attracts money and protection for the home; favors health and communication; it is a plant that stores negative vibes like a sponge and releases them at dusk.

Musk mallow

Malva moschata

Ruling Orisha: Shango
Element of Nature: Fire

Magical Classification: Male / Active

Increases luck and success and intuition, love, sensuality, and attraction between couples.

Mustard

Brassica juncea, Sinapsis alba
Liturgical Name: Ewéko
Ruling Orisha: Nana
Element of Nature: Water

Magical Classification: Female / Passive

Ensures the spiritual protection of Eshu; protects against theft; breaks envy and the evil eye.

Myrrh

Commiphora myrrha, Commiphora opobalsamum, Commiphora spp.
Ruling Orisha: Oshala
Element of Nature: Air

Magical Classification: Female / Passive

Wards off bad vibes and stimulates intuition; attracts good luck; in strong discharge, it repels evil spirits; facilitates contact with the spiritual planes.

Myrtle

Myrica cerifera
Ruling Orishas: Oshala, Oshun
Elements of Nature: Air, Water

Magical Classification: Female / Passive

Consolidates desires; strengthens and attracts love, passion, and seduction; brings brightness, success, recognition, and visibility.

Nalta jute

Other Popular Name: Jute mallow
Corchorus olitorius
Liturgical Name: Ewedu
Ruling Orisha: Omolu
Element of Nature: Earth

Magical Classification: Male / Active

Fabric made of its vines drives away poverty and breaks the force of physical and spiritual illnesses.

Negramina

Siparuna guianensis

Ruling Orishas: Yemaya, Obba, Shango

Magical Classification: Male / Active

Element of Nature: Fire

Used in recipes for discharging and spiritual cleansing.

Nettles

Laportea aestuans

Liturgical Names: Ewé Esisi, Ewé Kanan, Ewé Èpe

Ruling Orishas: Eshu

Element of Nature: Fire

Magical Classification: Male / Active

Used in recipes for discharging and spiritual cleansing.

Night-blooming jasmine

Cestrum nocturnum

Liturgical Name: Àlúkerésé

Ruling Orishas: Iyewa, Iansã, Oshun

Elements of Nature: Air, Water

Magical Classification: Female / Passive

Helps to find people with the same affinities; strengthens and attracts love, passion, and seduction.

Nut grass

Other Popular Names: Purple nutsedge, coco grass
Cyperus rotundus

Liturgical Name: Làbelàbe

Ruling Orishas: Eshu, Ogun, Shango

Element of Nature: Fire

Magical Classification: Male / Active

Attracts and strengthens prosperity and abundance; in powder form, along with other ingredients, it serves as a vanishing powder—to make someone leave home or work.

Nutmeg

Other Popular Name: Mace
Myristica fragrans, Myristicaceae fragrans

Liturgical Name: Àwùsá Òyìnbó

Ruling Orishas: Oshossi, Shango

Element of Nature: Earth, Fire

Magical Classification: Male / Active

Attracts wealth, suitable employment, and good company and partnerships; brings luck, fertility, and happiness.

Nuts

Carya illinoensis

Liturgical Name: Ariwò
Ruling Orishas: Oshala, Shango
Element of Nature: Fire

Magical Classification: Male /
Active

Brightens up the environment; attracts money and prosperity; attracts fertility and fecundity; promotes mediumship and clairvoyance.

Oak

Quercus boyacensis, Quercus colombiana, Quercus humboldtii, Quercus robur

Liturgical Names: Igi Apádò, Igi Óàkù
Ruling Orishas: Eshu, Ogun

Element of Nature: Earth
Magical Classification: Male /
Active

Attracts wisdom, money, and good luck; favors fertility and the home's maintenance and protection; brings strength, security, and courage to the paths.

Oats

Avena sativa

Ruling Orishas: Oshun, Oshossi
Elements of Nature: Earth, Water

Magical Classification: Female /
Passive

Attracts prosperity, money, abundance, and fertility; gives stability to plans and goals.

Olive

Olea europaea

Liturgical Name: Èso Oróro
Ruling Orisha: Shango
Element of Nature: Fire

Magical Classification: Male /
Active

Increases self-confidence; increases the power of attraction and sensuality; brings out the truth and helps in the search for justice.

Olive tree

Olea europaea

Ruling Orishas: Oshossi, Shango
Elements of Nature: Earth, Fire

Magical Classification: Male /
Active

Opens paths; attracts prosperity, abundance, and plentifulness; attracts good energies; strengthens leadership instincts.

Onion

Allium cepa

Liturgical Name: Àlùbósà   **Magical Classification:** Male /
Ruling Orisha: Eshu   Active
Element of Nature: Fire

Keeps away negative spirits and nightmares; brings protection to the house and prevents burglaries.

Orange

Citrus sinensis

Liturgical Name: Osán   **Magical Classification:** Female /
Ruling Orisha: Oshala   Passive
Element of Nature: Air

Relieves feelings of loneliness and abandonment; attracts love and promotes the acquisition of money and material goods; helps against insomnia and nervousness; favors mediumship and clairvoyance; brings harmony and calm.

Orange blossom

Citrus aurantium

Liturgical Name: Òrombó   **Element of Nature:** Air
Gaingain   **Magical Classification:** Female /
Ruling Orishas: Oshala   Passive

Wards off panic; increases security and self-confidence.

Orchid

Orchidaceae

Ruling Orisha: Oshala   **Magical Classification:** Female /
Element of Nature: Air   Passive

Balances thoughts and clears up ideas; recommended for purifying the work environment and helping to find solutions to practical everyday problems.

Oregano

Origanum vulgare

Ruling Orisha: Oshala   **Magical Classification:** Female /
Element of Nature: Air   Passive

Attracts and strengthens prosperity and abundance; attracts divine protection; puts an end to emotional suffering; brings harmony, peace, and psychic development.

Ornamental onion

Other Popular Names: Allium flowers, cebola-cencém
Allium spp.

Liturgical Name: Àlùbósà
Ruling Orishas: Eshu, Ogun
Elements of Nature: Fire, Earth

Magical Classification: Male /
Active

To discover falsehoods and betrayals and find lost objects, cut the onion into small pieces and, accompanied by the chants of Eshu, spread them in the corners of the rooms and under the furniture; it brings protection to the house.

Panacéia

Other Popular Names: Cipó-azougue, azougue-de-pobre
Apodanthera smilacifolia, Gomphrena arborescens, Sunanum cernuum

Ruling Orishas: Omolu, Shango
Elements of Nature: Earth, Fire

Magical Classification: Male /
Active

From it is made a powder that, spread to the surroundings, brings the improvement of financial conditions and attracts beneficial influences. However, this powder must be well-grounded in order not to cause the opposite effect; for spiritual cleansing, its fruit is cut into small pieces and spread throughout the house and under the furniture.

Paracress

Spilanthes acmella

Liturgical Name: Awure Pépé
Ruling Orisha: Oshun
Element of Nature: Water

Magical Classification: Female /
Passive

Attracts love, beauty, and courage to face the challenges of everyday life.

Passion fruit

Granadilla quadrangularis, Passiflora edulis, Passiflora macrocarpa, Passi-
flora quadrangularis

Liturgical Name: Kankinse
Ruling Orishas: Iyewa, Oshun,
Oshossi

Elements of Nature: Water,
Earth
Magical Classification: Female /
Passive

Helps to overcome the pain of loss and death; helps to react well in the face of grief and heartbreak; combats sadness and melancholy; in some cases, is used in love spells; reestablishes peace in friendships.

Patchouli

Pogostemon patchouly

Liturgical Name: Ewé Legbá

Ruling Orishas: Oshala, Oshun

Elements of Nature: Air, Water

Magical Classification: Female/ Passive

Sharpens intelligence; decreases mental confusion and indecision; stimulates love and seduction; favors fertility and fecundity; strengthens mediumship and spirituality.

Pau pereira

Other Popular Names: Tsunu, Indian snuff, rapé powder
Platycyamus regnellii

Ruling Orisha: Shango

Element of Nature: Fire

Magical Classification: Male/ Active

Attracts prosperity, abundance, and plentifulness; attracts harmony, peace, and peaceful thoughts; strengthens friendship.

Pea

Pisum sativum

Liturgical Names: Irú Èwà Òyìnbó Kan, Pòpòndò

Ruling Orisha: Oshun

Element of Nature: Water

Magical Classification: Female/ Passive

Attracts prosperity, abundance, and plentifulness; consolidates desires; strengthens and attracts love, passion, and seduction.

Peace lily

Lilium

Liturgical Name: Osumere

Ruling Orisha: Oshala

Element of Nature: Air

Magical Classification: Female/ Passive

It purifies and harmonizes environments, bringing peace and tranquility. In the bathroom, it is excellent for preventing the escape of energy through sink or shower drains.

Peach

Prunus persica
Liturgical Name: Egbesí   **Magical Classification:** Male /
Ruling Orisha: Shango   Active
Element of Nature: Fire

Opens paths; attracts prosperity, abundance, and plentifulness; favors fertility and fecundity; strengthens mediumship and spirituality; strengthens and attracts love.

Peanuts

Arachis hypogaea, Terminalia glaucescens
Liturgical Name: Èpà   **Magical Classification:** Male /
Ruling Orisha: Ossain   Active
Element of Nature: Earth

Strengthens sensuality and sexuality.

Pear

Pyrus communis
Ruling Orisha: Oshossi   **Magical Classification:** Male /
Element of Nature: Earth   Active

Opens paths; attracts prosperity, abundance, and plentifulness; favors fertility and fecundity; strengthens mediumship and spirituality; strengthens and attracts love, passion, and seduction.

Pencil cactus

Other Popular Name: Sticks on fire
Euphorbia tirucalli
Liturgical Name: Ikikigún   **Magical Classification:** Male /
Ruling Orisha: Eshu   Active
Element of Nature: Fire

Used in recipes for unloading and spiritual cleansing.

Pennyroyal

Mentha pulegium
Liturgical Name: Olátoríje   **Magical Classification:** Female /
Ruling Orishas: Iansã, Oshala   Passive
Element of Nature: Air

Keeps away the evil eye and envy; brings strength, courage, peace, and divine protection; used inside the soles of the shoes to help avoid physical and mental fatigue.

Pepper elder

Other Popular Names: Shining bush plant, alfavaca-roxa
Peperomia pellucida

Liturgical Name: Rínrín
Ruling Orishas: Yemaya, Oshala, Oshun

Elements of Nature: Air, Water
Magical Classification: Female/ Passive

Fights physical and emotional irritation; strengthens clairvoyance, broadens vision, and prevents seeing what does not need to be seen; reassures and sweetens outlook.

Peppermint

Mentha sativa, Mentha viridis

Ruling Orishas: Iansã, Oshala
Element of Nature: Air

Magical Classification: Female/ Passive

Relieves trauma and emotional shocks; good for health problems and emotional balance; recommended for increasing understanding and decision-making power.

Peregum (green or yellow)

Other Popular Names: Dracaena, dragon plant, corn plant
Dracaena fragrans

Liturgical Name: Ewé Pèrègún Ko
Ruling Orishas: Logunede, Oshossi

Element of Nature: Earth
Magical Classification: Male/ Active

Opens paths; attracts good energies; strengthens mediumship and spirituality; brings strength and courage to face challenges.

Peruvian pepper tree

Schinus molle

Liturgical Name: Àjóbi Oilé
Ruling Orishas: Eshu, Ogun, Oshossi

Element of Nature: Earth
Magical Classification: Male/ Active

Used in recipes for discharging and spiritual cleansing.

Pichury bean

Nectandra pichury

Ruling Orishas: Oshala, Oshun
Elements of Nature: Air, Water

Magical Classification: Female/ Passive

Cancels negative vibes; provides spiritual protection.

Pine

Pinus sylvestris

Ruling Orishas: Ossain, Oshossi   **Magical Classification:** Male /
Element of Nature: Earth   Active

Opens paths; attracts prosperity, abundance, and plentifulness; favors fertility and fecundity; strengthens mediumship and spirituality.

Pineapple

Ananas comosus

Liturgical Names: Ekúnkún   **Ruling Orishas:** Ogun, Oshossi
Ahùn, Eékún Ahùn, Ògèdè   **Element of Nature:** Earth
Òyìnbó, Òpe Òyìnbó, Òpòn   **Magical Classification:** Male /
Òyìnbó   Active

Attracts people's generosity; excellent to fight greed; strengthens friendships; brings prosperity and good luck.

Pink trumpet tree

Other Popular Names: Pink ipê, pink lapacho, ipê-poui tree
Handroanthus impetiginosus

Ruling Orishas: Nana, Omolu   **Magical Classification:** Female /
Elements of Nature: Earth,   Passive
Water

Opens paths, helps against insomnia and nervousness, balances emotions, and relieves trauma and emotional shocks; brings harmony and calm to thoughts.

Pixirica

Other Popular Name: Tapixirica
Leandra australis

Ruling Orishas: Eshu, Shango   **Magical Classification:** Male /
Element of Nature: Fire   Active

Makes an excellent powder that allows the solution of problems; strengthens mediumship and spirituality.

Plantain

Plantago major, Plantago tomentoso
Liturgical Names: Ewé Òpá
Ruling Orisha: Ogun
Element of Nature: Earth

Magical Classification: Male /
Active

Opens paths; attracts good energies; strengthens mediumship and spirituality; brings strength and courage.

Poinsettia

Euphorbia pulcherrima
Ruling Orisha: Ogun
Element of Nature: Earth

Magical Classification: Male /
Active

Brings strength and courage to face challenges.

Pokeweed

Phytolacca americana
Ruling Orisha: Eshu
Element of Nature: Fire

Magical Classification: Male /
Active

Used in recipes for spiritual discharging.

Pomegranate

Punica granatum
Liturgical Name: Àgbá
Ruling Orisha: Shango
Element of Nature: Fire

Magical Classification: Male /
Active

Opens paths; attracts prosperity, abundance, and plentifulness; attracts good energies; strengthens leadership.

Pond apple

Other Popular Names: Alligator apple, swamp apple
Annona glabra
Liturgical Name: Àfe
Ruling Orishas: Yemaya, Omolu, Oshumare

Elements of Nature: Earth, Water
Magical Classification: Male /
Active

Used in recipes for unloading and spiritual cleansing.

Poplar

Populus nigra

Ruling Orishas: Ogun, Oshossi, Shango

Magical Classification: Male / Active

Elements of Nature: Earth, Fire

Assists in astral projection exercises, brings prosperity, and is excellent for those looking for a new job or professional promotion.

Poppy

Papaver somniferum

Ruling Orishas: Iansã, Oshun

Magical Classification: Female / Passive

Element of Nature: Water

Opens paths; attracts prosperity, abundance, and plentifulness; favors fertility and fecundity; strengthens and attracts love, passion, and seduction.

Porangaba

Other Popular Name: Cordia
Cordia salicifolia

Liturgical Name: Igi Òmò

Magical Classification: Male / Active

Ruling Orisha: Ogun

Element of Nature: Earth

Helps overcome relationship breakdowns; brings strength and courage to face challenges.

Potato

Ipomoea batatas

Liturgical Names: Ànàmó, Òdùkún

Element of Nature: Earth

Ruling Orisha: Oshossi

Magical Classification: Male / Active

Attracts prosperity and abundance; strengthens male and female fertility; brings security in decisions.

Prickly ash

Other Popular Names: Mamica de cadela, tambataru
Zanthoxylum rhoifolium

Liturgical Name: Igi Àta

Magical Classification: Male/
Active

Ruling Orisha: Eshu

Element of Nature: Fire

Used in recipes for discharge and spiritual cleansing.

Pumpkin

Cucurbita pepo

Liturgical Name: Élégédé

Element of Nature: Earth

Ruling Orishas: Logunede,
Oshossi

Magical Classification: Male/
Active

Attracts prosperity, material wealth, and happiness; attracts good luck and unveils secrets; brings security in words and increases the power of persuasion.

Punarnava

Other Popular Names: Red spiderling, spreading hogweed, tar vine
Boerhavia difussa

Liturgical Name: Etìpólà

Magical Classification: Female/
Passive

Ruling Orishas: Iansã, Logunede

Element of Nature: Water

Its roots are used in enchantments to increase spiritual strength and, especially, so that a novice does not flee from magical initiation rituals, establishing bonds of commitment to the sacred.

Purging nut

Other Popular Names: Physic nut, Barbados nut
Jatropha curcas

Liturgical Name: Bòtújè Funfun

Magical Classification: Male/
Active

Ruling Orisha: Eshu

Element of Nature: Fire

This plant has the incredible power to break spells; used in recipes for discharging and spiritual cleansing.

Purple basil

Ocimum basilicum

Liturgical Names: Efinrin Pupá, Efinrín, Efinrín Ata
Ruling Orishas: Iansã, Omolu

Elements of Nature: Fire, Earth
Magical Classification: Male/Active

Used in recipes for discharging and spiritual cleansing.

Purple orchid tree

Other Popular Names: Purple bauhinia, orchid tree
Bauhinia purpurea

Ruling Orisha: Yemaya
Element of Nature: Water

Magical Classification: Female/Passive

Used in recipes for discharging and spiritual cleansing.

Purslane

Portulaca oleracea

Liturgical Name: Ségúnsété
Ruling Orishas: Eshu, Omolu
Elements of Nature: Earth, Fire

Magical Classification: Male/Active

Attracts prosperity, wealth, and happiness; brings confidence in words and increases the power of persuasion.

Quince

Cydonia oblonga

Ruling Orisha: Eshu
Element of Nature: Fire

Magical Classification: Male/Active

Helps to overcome the pain of loss and death; helps to react well in the face of grief and disgust; excellent for spiritual cleansing; facilitates learning and improves the ability to learn; improves public speaking and the ability to make speeches.

Raspberry

Rubus idaeus

Liturgical Name: Éyà Àgbáyun Kan
Ruling Orisha: Iansã

Element of Nature: Fire
Magical Classification: Male/Active

Opens paths; attracts good energies; attracts love, passion, and seduction; strengthens mediumship and spirituality; strengthens friendships and social relationships.

Rattleweed

Other Popular Names: Devil-bean, shack shack, wedge-leaf rattlepod
Crotalaria retusa

Liturgical Name: Ewé Ìsin
Ruling Orisha: Eshu
Element of Nature: Fire

Magical Classification: Male /
Atctivation

Used in recipes for discharging and spiritual cleansing.

Rose apple

Other Popular Name: Malabar plum
Syzygium jambos

Liturgical Name: Igi Èso Pupa
Ruling Orisha: Ogun
Element of Nature: Earth

Magical Classification: Male /
Active

Opens paths; helps to react well to sorrow and disgust; brings strength and courage to face challenges.

Rosemary

Rosmarinus officinais

Liturgical Names: Ewéré,
Sawéwé
Ruling Orisha: Oshala

Element of Nature: Air
Magical Classification: Female /
Passive

Wards off thieves and protects the home; fights sadness and melancholy; defends against spiritual illness; removes envy and the evil eye and protects from spells; stimulates concentration, memory, and studies; brings happiness.

Rough-leaved pepper

Other Popular Names: Betis-cheiroso, jaborandi-manso
Piper amalago

Liturgical Name: Ewé Boyi
Ruling Orishas: Yemaya, Oshala
Elements of Nature: Air, Water

Magical Classification: Female /
Passive

Attracts harmony, peace, and peaceful thoughts; excellent in spiritual purification; strengthens friendships.

Royal poinciana

Other Popular Names: Flamboyant, flame tree
Delonix regia

Liturgical name: Sekeseke
Ruling Orishas: Iansã, Oshun
Element of Nature: Water

Magical Classification: Female /
Passive

Conolidates desires; excellent in love and sexual spells; favors fertility and fecundity; strengthens mediumship and spirituality; strengthens love.

Rue

Ruta graveolens

Liturgical Name: Atopá Kun
Ruling Orisha: Eshu
Element of Nature: Fire

Magical Classification: Male /
Active

Relieves trauma and emotional shock; amulet protects against the evil eye; excellent against bad influences and the evil eye; intensifies willpower, helping the person using it to fulfill their desires; brings spiritual protection and cuts negative currents.

Rushfoil

Croton heliotropiifolius

Ruling Orisha: Omolu
Element of Nature: Earth

Magical Classification: Male /
Active

Used in recipes for discharging and spiritual cleansing.

Rye

Secale cereale

Ruling Orishas: Oshun, Oshossi
Element of Nature: Earth

Magical Classification: Male /
Active

Stimulates love, truth, loyalty, and fidelity.

Saffron

Bixa orellana, Crocus sativus, Curcuma longa

Liturgical Name: Òsùn Buke
Ruling Orishas: Oshossi, Shango
Elements of Nature: Earth, Fire

Magical Classification: Male /
Active

Attracts prosperity, material wealth, and happiness; brings security in words and increases persuasive power.

Sage
Salvia divinorum, Salvia officinalis
Liturgical Name: Irikiwí   **Magical Classification:** Female /
Ruling Orisha: Oshala   Passive
Element of Nature: Air

Gives behavior and words serenity; strengthens self-confidence in interviews, meetings, and hearings; cleanses the environment and body of negative energies; brings wisdom; and favors the fulfillment of desires.

Sandalwood
Santalum album
Liturgical Name: Ewé Didún   **Magical Classification:** Male /
Ruling Orishas: Oshun, Oshossi   Active
Element of Nature: Earth

Opens paths; attracts prosperity, abundance, and plenty; favors fertility and fecundity; strengthens mediumship and spirituality.

Sarsaparille
Other Popular Names: Rough bindweed, smilax
Smilax aspera
Ruling Orishas: Iansã, Oshun   **Magical Classification:** Male /
Element of Nature: Fire   Active

Attracts money, abundance, and prosperity; consolidates desires; makes a powder with cinnamon and sandalwood to attract good customers and new business; strengthens and attracts love, passion, and seduction; brings radiance and brilliance.

Scratchbush
Urera baccifera
Liturgical Name: Ewé Ajofa   **Magical Classification:** Male /
Ruling Orisha: Eshu   Active
Element of Nature: Fire

Used in recipes for discharging and spiritual cleansing.

Senna alata

Other Popular Name: Candle bush
Cassia alata, Senna alata

Liturgical Name: Asunwon   **Magical Classification:** Male /
Ruling Orisha: Eshu   Active
Element of Nature: Fire

Used in recipes for discharging and spiritual cleansing.

Sensitive plant

Other Popular Names: Humble plant, shame plant, touch-me-not
Mimosa pudica, Terminalia superba

Liturgical Names: Afàrà, Apèjè,   **Element of Nature:** Water
Patonmó   **Magical Classification:** Female /
Ruling Orishas: Iansã, Nana   Passive

Opens the channels of spiritual communication and clairvoyance; eliminates negative energies; strengthens mediumship and spirituality.

Sesame

Sesamum indicum

Liturgical Names: Ekú Igi,   **Element of Nature:** Earth
Yànmótí   **Magical Classification:** Female /
Ruling Orishas: Oshun, Oshossi   Passive

Opens paths; helps attract friends, customers, and money; unlocks doors; makes what is not seen shine; stimulates creativity and joy.

Shea

Butyrospermum parkii, Vitellaria paradoxa

Liturgical Names: Emi, Òrí   **Magical Classification:** Female /
Ruling Orisha: Oshala   Passive
Element of Nature: Water

The leaves of this tree, and especially the shea butter extracted from its nuts, are fundamental to the cult of Ori—the spiritual head—representing the divine and creative power that gives life and allows the continuation of matter.

Shrubby false buttonweed

Borreria verticillata

Liturgical Name: Iràwò Ilè
Ruling Orishas: Eshu, Oshun
Elements of Nature: Water, Fire

Magical Classification: Female / Passive

Used in recipes for discharging and spiritual cleansing.

Silver cecropia

Cecropia hololeuca, Cecropia palmata

Liturgical Name: Àgbaó
Ruling Orishas: Yemaya, Nana, Shango

Elements of Nature: Water, Fire
Magical Classification: Female / Passive

Assists in objectives; makes you find what you are looking for.

Sleepy morning

Waltheria indica

Liturgical Name: Ewé Epo
Ruling Orisha: Oshun
Element of Nature: Water

Magical Classification: Female / Passive

Attracts prosperity, abundance, and plentifulness; helps to react well in the face of sorrow and disgust.

Slender amaranth

Amaranthus viridis

Liturgical Name: Tètè
Ruling Orishas: Yemaya, Oshala
Elements of Nature: Air, Water

Magical Classification: Female / Passive

Harmonizes the eye and increases clairvoyance; brings security and self-confidence.

Snake plant

Other Popular Names: St. George's sword, mother-in-law's tongue
Sansevieria trifasciata

Liturgical Name: Ewé Idà Orísa
Ruling Orishas: Ogun, Oshossi
Element of Nature: Fire

Magical Classification: Male / Active

It rids the person from other people's chatter and gossip; optimum spiritual protection against negative energies in body cleansings.

Soapbush

Clidemia hirta

Liturgical Names: Ewé Inà, Ewé Inón

Ruling Orishas: Eshu, Iansã, Shango

Element of Nature: Fire

Magical Classification: Male/Active

In small portions, it stimulates desires and provides a boost of movement for achieving goals; used in recipes for discharging and spiritual cleansing.

Sorrel

Oxalis acetosella

Liturgical Name: Isapá Funfun

Ruling Orishas: Oshun, Shango

Elements of Nature: Fire, Water

Magical Classification: Male/Active

Attracts love, seduction, beauty, and sympathy.

Soursop

Annona muricata

Liturgical Names: Èkò Omodé, Èkò Òyìnbó

Ruling Orishas: Yemaya, Oshumare

Element of Nature: Water

Magical Classification: Female/Passive

Used in recipes for discharging and spiritual cleansing.

Spanish cedar

Cedrela odorata

Liturgical Name: Igi Òpepe

Ruling Orishas: Ogun, Oshossi

Element of Nature: Earth

Magical Classification: Male/Active

Attracts money, protection, and strength; stimulates psychic strength.

Spearmint

Other Popular Name: Garden mint
Mentha spicata

Liturgical Name: Eré Túntún   **Magical Classification:** Female /
Ruling Orishas: Ogun, Oshala   Passive
Elements of Nature: Earth, Air

Opens paths; helps against insomnia and nervousness; balances emotions and relieves trauma and emotional shock; brings strength and courage to face challenges; brings harmony and calm to thoughts.

Spider flower

Cleome hassleriana

Ruling Orisha: Eshu   **Magical Classification:** Male /
Element of Nature: Fire   Active

Used in recipes for discharging and spiritual cleansing.

Spider plant

Chlorophytum comosum

Ruling Orishas: Eshu, Ogun   **Magical Classification:** Male /
Elements of Nature: Earth, Fire   Active

Protects passages and entrances in the place where it is planted; brings strength and courage to face challenges.

Spiked spiralflag ginger

Other Popular Name: Indianhead ginger
Costus spicatus

Liturgical Name: Tetèrègún   **Magical classification:** Female /
Ruling Orishas: Yemaya, Ogun   Passive
Element of Nature: Water

Makes the person understand others' opinions; brings balance to the head, avoiding anguish and melancholy.

Spiny amaranth
Other Popular Names: Spiny pigweed, prickly amaranth, thorny amaranth
Amaranthus spinosus
Liturgical Name: Tètè Elégun
Ruling Orisha: Eshu
Element of Nature: Fire
Magical Classification: Male/ Active

It is a magical weapon, used for physical and spiritual defense, breaking spells and curses and bringing insecurity and danger to those who do evil.

Spiral ginger
Costus guanaiensis, Rumex hymenosepalus
Ruling Orishas: Iyewa, Nana, Ogun, Oshossi
Elements of Nature: Earth, Water
Magical Classification: Male/ Active

Opens paths; helps to react well in the face of hurt and heartbreak; brings strength and courage to face challenges.

Star anise
Illicium verum
Ruling Orishas: Oshun, Oshossi
Elements of Nature: Earth, Water
Magical Classification: Male/ Active

Favors good luck and love; promotes good friendships.

Strawberry
Fragaria ananassa, Fragaria schiloensis, Fragaria vesca
Liturgical Name: Irú Èso Dídùn Kan
Ruling Orisha: Shango
Element of Nature: Fire
Magical Classification: Male/ Active

Helps overcome the pain of loss and breakups of relationships; relieves loneliness and abandonment; attracts good luck; excellent in the magic of love and sex.

Strawberry guava

Other Popular Names: Cattley guava
Psidium cattleyanum

Liturgical Name: Ejà Omoodé
Ruling Orishas: Yemaya, Oshun, Oshossi

Elements of Nature: Earth, Water
Magical Classification: Male/Active

Used in recipes for spiritual purification.

Sugarcane

Saccharum officinarum

Liturgical Names: Ikésén, Ìrèké
Ruling Orishas: Eshu, Oshala
Elements of Nature: Fire, Air

Magical Classification: Male/Active

Its dried leaves and pulp are used in fumigations to purify the environment; it attracts pleasant circumstances; its derivatives—sugarcane juice and brown sugar—are used in rituals to bring sweetness, happiness, love, and prosperity.

Surinam cherry

Other Popular Names: Brazilian cherry, pitanga
Eugenia uniflora

Liturgical Name: Ewé Ítà
Ruling Orisha: Iansã
Element of Nature: Fire

Magical Classification: Male/Active

Opens paths; attracts good energies; attracts love; strengthens mediumship; strengthens friendships.

Surinam cherry blossom

Eugenia uniflora

Liturgical Name: Ítà
Ruling Orisha: Iansã
Element of Nature: Fire

Magical Classification: Male/Active

Favors agreements and companies; powerful in rituals related to financial issues; promotes material acquisitions and successful negotiations.

Sweet goldenrod
Solidago odora

Liturgical Name: Bánjókó
Ruling Orishas: Eshu, Oshun
Element of Nature: Fire

Magical Classification: Male / Active

Eliminates negative energies from the environment; promotes fertility and fecundity; strengthens mediumship and spirituality; and brings divinatory dreams.

Sweet potato
Ipomoea batatas

Liturgical Name: Kúnkúndùnkú
Ruling Orishas: Iyewa, Oshumare

Element of Nature: Earth
Magical Classification: Male / Active

Encourages that all parts of a group, ensemble, or society receive equal attention; its leaves bring emotional and spiritual balance.

Sweetgum
Liquidambar styraciflua

Ruling Orishas: Omolu, Oshala
Elements of Nature: Air, Earth

Magical Classification: Male / Active

The powder made with its resin and mixed with benzoin is used in fumigations intended for purification and breaking curses.

Sycamore fig
Ficus sycomorus

Ruling Orishas: Omolu, Oshala
Elements of Nature: Air, Earth

Magical Classification: Male / Active

Attracts prosperity, abundance, and plentifulness; attracts harmony, peace, and peaceful thoughts; strengthens friendships and social relationships.

Tabasco pepper
Capsicum frutescens

Ruling Orisha: Ogun
Element of Nature: Earth

Magical Classification: Male / Active

Used in recipes for discharging and spiritual cleansing.

Tarragon

Artemisia dracunculus

Ruling Orishas: Eshu, Ogun, Shango

Magical Classification: Male / Active

Element of Nature: Fire

Provides courage and strength; makes you have command over another person; strengthens self-confidence.

Tayuya

Cayaponia tayuya

Liturgical Names: Dòtánù, Wòmìrìn, Àkútàpá

Ruling Orisha: Eshu

Element of Nature: Fire

Magical Classification: Male / Active

The branch is used to surround rituals of defense, like a crown; used in recipes for discharge.

Tea plant

Camellia sinensis

Ruling Orishas: Yemaya, Oshossi, Omolu

Magical Classification: Female / Passive

Elements of Nature: Water, Earth

Helps overcome relationship breakdowns.

Thyme

Thymus vulgaris

Liturgical Name: Efinrín Wéwé

Ruling Orisha: Oshossi

Element of Nature: Earth

Magical Classification: Male / Active

Opens paths; attracts prosperity, abundance, and plenty; favors fertility and fecundity; strengthens and attracts love, passion, and seduction.

Tibouchina tree

Other Popular Name: Glory bush
Tibouchina mutabilis

Ruling Orisha: Oshossi

Element of Nature: Earth

Magical Classification: Male / Active

Its foot and stump are appropriate places to put down obligations and offerings of prosperity and abundance.

Tomato

Lycopersicon esculentum

Liturgical Name: Tòmátì

Ruling Orishas: Iansã, Oshossi, Shango

Elements of Nature: Fire, Earth

Magical Classification: Male / Active

Consolidates desires; strengthens and attracts love.

Tonka beans

Other Popular Name: Cumaru

Coumarouna odorata, Coumarouna tetraphylla, Dipteryx odorata

Ruling Orisha: Oshala

Element of Nature: Air

Magical Classification: Female / Calm

The powder made with its fruit is used in fumigations or simply spread in the environment, canceling out negative vibes and chasing away evil spirits.

Toothache plant

Acmella oleracea, Spilanthes acmella, Spilanthes oleracea

Liturgical Name: Oripépe

Ruling Orisha: Oshun

Element of Nature: Water

Magical Classification: Female / Passive

Sharpens intelligence; attracts harmony, peace, and quiet thoughts; lessens mental confusion and indecision; stimulates love and seduction; strengthens friendships.

Tree cotton

Gossypium arboreum

Liturgical Names: Akese, Owù

Ruling Orisha: Oshala

Element of Nature: Air

Magical Classification: Female / Passive

Illuminates the paths; cleanses wounds and the wounds of the soul; purifies the mind and thoughts.

Tropical milkweed

Asclepias curassavica

Ruling Orisha: Ogun

Element of Nature: Earth

Magical Classification: Male / Active

Opens paths; attracts good energies; provides good ways, courage, and strength to win wars and the challenges of destiny; strengthens leadership instincts.

Vanilla

Vanilla fragrans, Vanilla planifolia

Liturgical Name: Àbàrà Òké

Ruling Orishas: Ossain, Oshun

Elements of Nature: Water, Earth

Magical Classification: Female/Passive

Attracts love, seduction, and beauty; favors sympathy and recognition.

Vetiver

Chrysopogon zizanioides

Ruling Orishas: Eshu, Oshun, Oshossi

Elements of Nature: Fire, Earth

Magical Classification: Male/Active

Protects commerce, favoring good sales, attracting money and good luck; used for meditation, inspiration, and soothing the body and mind.

Violet

Saintpaulia ionantha

Ruling Orishas: Nana, Oshala

Elements of Nature: Air, Water

Magical Classification: Female/Passive

Scares off negative energy; facilitates concentration and meditation; harmonizes coexistence among people; and stimulates self-confidence.

Water hyacinth

Eichhornia crassipes

Liturgical Name: Ejá Omodé

Ruling Orishas: Nana, Oshun

Element of Nature: Water

Magical Classification: Female/Passive

Opens paths; attracts prosperity, abundance, and plenty; facilitates obtaining favors and advantages; favors fertility and fecundity; strengthens mediumship and spirituality.

Water lettuce

Pistia stratiotes

Liturgical Name: Ojúoró

Ruling Orishas: Iyewa, Yemaya, Ossain, Oshun

Element of Nature: Water

Magical Classification: Female/Calm

Attracts love and seduction; gives eloquence in words; strengthens mediumship and spirituality; brings recognition and individual brilliance.

Watermelon

Citrulus vulgaris

Liturgical Name: Bàrà

Ruling Orishas: Eshu, Yemaya, Oshun

Elements of Nature: Fire, Water

Magical Classification: Female / Passive

Sharpens intelligence; attracts prosperity, abundance, and plenty; lessens mental confusion and indecision; gives radiance and recognition; stimulates love and seduction.

Wheat

Triticum vulgare

Liturgical Name: Oká

Ruling Orisha: Oshossi

Element of Nature: Earth

Magical Classification: Male / Active

Opens paths; attracts prosperity, abundance, and plenty; attracts good energies; strengthens leadership instincts.

White angel's trumpet

Brugmansia suaveolens

Liturgical Name: Antijuí

Ruling Orisha: Oshala

Element of Nature: Air

Magical Classification: Female / Passive

Used in recipes for discharging and spiritual cleansing.

White corn

Zea mays

Liturgical Name: Àgbado Funfun

Ruling Orisha: Oshala

Element of Nature: Air

Magical Classification: Female / Passive

Symbol of peace, softness, and protection of beings superior to humanity.

White rose

Rosa alba, Rosa centifolia

Ruling Orisha: Oshala

Element of Nature: Air

Magical Classification: Female / Passive

Helps react well in the face of hurt and heartbreak; strengthens spirituality; brings strength and courage.

White sandalwood

Santalum album

Liturgical Name: Ewé Didún Funfun

Ruling Orisha: Oshala

Element of Nature: Air

Magical Classification: Female/Passive

Increases the power of meditation and magical concentration; excellent for spiritual protection; brings success and personal recognition.

White water lily

Nymphaea alba

Liturgical Name: Òsíbàtá

Ruling Orishas: Iyewa, Oshala, Oshun

Element of Nature: Water

Magical Classification: Female/Passive

Attracts love and seduction; gives eloquence to words; strengthens mediumship and spirituality; brings recognition and personal brilliance.

White willow

Salix alba, Salix alba tristis

Ruling Orishas: Omolu, Oshun

Elements of Nature: Earth, Water

Magical Classification: Male/Active

Opens paths; attracts good energies; attracts love.

Whitebrush

Aloysia gratissima

Liturgical Name: Àrùsò

Ruling Orishas: Yemaya, Oshala, Oshun

Elements of Nature: Air, Water

Magical Classification: Female/Passive

Calms, purifies, and brings understanding, balance, and harmony among people; favors family love, good luck, and spiritual protection in all aspects; cleanses the environment.

Whitewort

Leucas martinicensis

Liturgical Name: Moborò

Ruling Orisha: Iansã

Element of Nature: Fire

Magical Classification: Female/Passive

Strengthens spirituality and connection with the sacred.

Wild custard apple

Annona senegalensis

Liturgical Name: Àbo

Ruling Orishas: Yemaya, Omolu, Oshumare

Elements of Nature : Earth, Water

Magical Classification: Male / Active

Used in recipes for unloading and spiritual cleansing.

Wild fig

Ficus thonningi

Liturgical Name: Ódàn

Ruling Orisha: Eshu

Element of Nature: Fire

Magical Classification: Male / Active

Helps to get rid of debts; establishes contact between the physical and the supernatural world; favors fertility and fecundity; makes decisions for those who use it; strengthens mediumship.

Wild mint

Other Popular Name: Field mint
Mentha arvensis

Ruling Orishas: Eshu, Omolu

Element of Nature: Earth

Magical Classification: Male / Active

Used in recipes for spiritual discharging.

Wild sunflower

Other Popular Name: Hemorrhage plant
Aspilia africana, Tithonia diversifolia

Liturgical Names: Agbale, Jogbo, Yinrin-yinrin, Yúnriun, Yúnyún, Ákò Yúnyún

Ruling Orishas: Oshala, Oshun

Elements of Nature: Air, Fire

Magical Classification: Female / Passive

Opens paths; attracts brightness and recognition, prosperity, and abundance; favors fertility and fecundity; strengthens mediumship and spirituality; strengthens and attracts love, passion, and seduction.

Willow-leaved justicia

Justicia gendarussa

Ruling Orisha: Ogun

Element of Nature: Earth

Magical Classification: Male/Active

Cancels spells and negative energies; brings strength and courage to face challenges.

Wine palm

Other Popular Names: Raffia palm, West African piassava palm, African bamboo palm

Raphia vinifera

Liturgical Name: Ikó

Ruling Orishas: Nana, Omolu, Oshala

Elements of Nature: Air, Earth

Magical Classification: Male/Active

It has the power to hide something; it is used as protection against evil energies and malicious spirits; it is the garment of Omolu, the lord of healing and diseases, who is also the Orisha responsible for the separation of the spirit from the body at the time of the disincarnation.

Wing-stem camphorweed

Pluchea sagittalis

Liturgical Name: Obalu

Ruling Orishas: Nana, Omolu

Elements of Nature: Water, Earth

Magical Classification: Male/Active

Used in recipes for discharging and spiritual cleansing.

Wireweed

Other Popular Name: Malva-do-campo

Sida macrodon

Liturgical Names: Efin, Àsíkùtá

Ruling Orishas: Oshala, Oshossi

Elements of Nature: Earth, Air

Magical Classification: Female/Passive

Brings strength and courage to face challenges.

Wolfsbane

Other Popular Name: Monkshood
Aconitum napellus

Ruling Orisha: Eshu

Element of Nature: Fire

Magical Classification: Male / Active

It is made into a powder that, when blown onto a person's feet, back, or shadow, causes them to disappear from your path; excellent for warding off negative energies.

Yam

Dioscorea alata, Dioscorea cayennensis, Dioscorea rotundata

Liturgical Names: Arufanfan, Duduku, Ewura, Ewura Funfun, Ewura Pupa, Igángan, Isu, Isu Ewura, Isu Ode, Ègbódo, Òdo

Ruling Orishas: Ogun, Oshoguian

Element of Nature: Earth

Magical Classification: Male / Active

Opens paths to success and progress; acts especially on male fertility and fecundity, but also on female fertility and fecundity; its leaves are used in the magic of love and union, whether of couples or families.

Yarrow

Achillea millefolium

Ruling Orisha: Oshala

Element of Nature: Air

Magical Classification: Female / Passive

Consolidates desires; excellent for job interviews and important meetings; favors social relations; strengthens and attracts love, passion, and seduction.

Herbal Grimoire

Grimoire is the name given to books of magic that bring together teachings on the manipulation of the forces of nature, recipes for rituals and incantations, and secrets and mysteries of various magical and spiritual traditions around the world. A few centuries ago, people used to keep these books under lock and key, such was the importance of the knowledge contained in them.

Nature has hundreds of thousands of plant species, and it would be impossible to create a complete list of all existing species and their magical properties. More than that, if we were to write and print this list, believe me, you would have in your hands not one but countless heavy volumes of an endless encyclopedia. And let's be honest, it is neither my intention nor my claim to encapsulate the truth of all world's plants in the words that make up this work. Yet, with deep affection and gratitude, I share with you a little of what I have learned and wish that this knowledge will be as useful to you as it has been for me all these years.

The dictionary of magical herbs in the previous section is an attempt to gather a little of all this knowledge. Yet, so that you can begin performing your spells, I have selected some for which I have a special affection. All these recipes are already balanced, ready to be applied wherever and whenever you wish. However, to give them your personal touch, I purposely left out a little something: the incantation to *awaken* the power of each leaf used in these recipes. So when performing your rituals with baths and fumigations, or when creating your power pots and Roma pots, focus on your purpose, visualize and set your best intentions, and let your intuition flow to compose your words of power: I believe in your transforming potential, and I know that *you can sing to enchant!*

Spiritual Cleansing and Defense

Cleansing Bath

- Basil leaves
- Colônia or spiral ginger leaves
- Rue leaves

In 2 liters of water, boil all the leaves, cover, and let cool. Take this bath from the neck down.

Defense Bath

- Gale-of-the-wind leaves
- Dumb cane leaves
- Basil leaves
- Peppermint leaves
- Abre-caminho fern branches
- 1 snake plant cut into 7 pieces

In 2 liters of water, boil all the leaves, cover, and let cool. Take this bath from the neck down.

Discharge Bath

- Guinea hen weed leaves
- Nettles or soapbush leaves
- Spearmint leaves
- 1 bottle of *cachaça* (sugarcane liquor), rum, or other spirits

In 2 liters of water, boil all the leaves, cover them up, and let them cool. Mix in the bottle of spirits and take from the neck down.

Attention: This bath should only be taken in extreme cases, as its energy is highly active and concentrated.

The Blue Ritual: Homemade Exorcism

Taking care of yourself and taking care of your personal space and where you live are activities full of symbolism: our home is a reflection of ourselves. It's no wonder that when our house is well cared for, clean, and smells good, with everything in its place, we feel more confident and more alive—sometimes even happier. This is true in the physical world and in the spiritual world: taking care of yourself and your home reflects and echoes in the astral world.

Therefore, just as it is necessary to clean and maintain the physical cleanliness of your home, it is also important from time to time to perform an energetic cleaning of you and your family, eliminating the negative energies that accumulate like dust in the rooms. As time goes on, these energies begin to interfere in your day-to-day life; they alter your mood, suck at your disposition and self-esteem, affect the sleep of children and adults, and provoke fights and general discomfort. The Blue Ritual is a powerful and very effective way to purify your home's environment and drive away bad energies. And best of all, you can accomplish it whenever you wish! However, it is important to remember that pregnant women, children, and people with poor health should not perform it or be present in the place where you are performing it.

Note: All the sprays listed below, as well as ready-to-use baths and African black soap, can be purchased at www.diegodeoxossi .com.br/shop and delivered worldwide.

Materials Needed

- White adhesive tape
- Bucket and washcloth
- 2 handfuls of coarse salt
- 1 light blue candle
- 1 Blue Purification Spray
- 1 Golden Prosperity Spray
- African black soap or coconut soap
- 1 spiritual defense bath

How to Perform the Ritual

1. On the morning of the day you will complete the ritual, cover your navel (where the solar plexus is, the most important chakra in your body) with a piece of white tape, protecting it from harmful energies.

2. Do a complete physical cleaning of the environment you want to purify: clean everything, throw away what is broken no longer useful, and separate the clothes you no longer wear and donate them.

3. Then mix in a bucket: 2 liters of pure water and 5 tablespoons of the Blue Purification Spray.

4. Before starting the Blue Ritual, place the two handfuls of coarse salt on the floor at the main entrance door. It must be on the inside—one on each side, on the left and on the right.

5. With a clean washcloth, soak it in the prepared mixture, wring it out, and wipe it over every room in the house, from the back to the main entrance door; if there is more than one floor in the place, always start at the highest floor and work down to the ground floor.

6. Remember to also clean furniture, glass, pottery, and especially tiles; when you're done, set the bucket with what's left of the water near the main entrance door of your house.

7. Continuing the ritual, in the same direction that you performed the cleaning with the washcloth—from the back to the main door—spray the Blue Purification Spray on the walls, in the corners, on the doorjambs, and in the dark corners behind the sinks and stoves (as it is there that the negative energy is most concentrated).

8. Arriving back at the main entrance door again, collect the coarse salt that was left on the floor along with the water from the bucket. Pour whatever is left over from the ritual onto the street in front of your house.

If you wish, you can complement the spiritual cleansing of your home or business by using the Golden Prosperity Spray.

Finishing Up the Ritual

Light a light blue candle and imagine the candlelight expanding throughout the purified place, illuminating and harmonizing the environment and the people who live in it. Instead of regular soap, use African black soap or coconut soap to lather up. Rinse the soap off with water from the shower, and then, from the neck down, take your spiritual defense bath. After bathing, remove the tape from your navel and throw it in the trash.

Green Ritual: Breaks Envy

We live in a society and, as a result, we interact with all possible kinds of people: happy or sad, polite or rude, calm or anxious. Besides this, the modern world makes conflict a constant in our lives, and, even without wanting to, we are subject to the frustrations of others and their effects on us. Just as the Blue Ritual is an excellent "spiritual cleanser" for physical spaces, when we feel drained by the energies of the places around us or by the influence of obsessive spirits on them, the Green Ritual is a powerful personal protection that destroys envy, trouble, and the evil eye.

Materials Needed

- 1 common dinner plate
- White paper and pencil
- 1 large handful of coarse salt
- 1 piece of charcoal
- 1 dark green candle
- 1 Green Spiritual Defense Spray
- African black soap or coconut soap
- 1 spiritual defense bath

How to Perform the Ritual

1. On white paper, write down your full name and date of birth seven times in pencil. Place the paper in the middle of the plate and, on top of it, place the piece of charcoal.

2. Around the paper, on the plate, make a circle of coarse salt. Next to the paper with your name on it, inside the salt circle, light the green candle and visualize its light expanding and illuminating your body, entering through your chakras and expelling envy and the evil eye from you. See the rays of green light growing throughout the purified place, illuminating

and harmonizing the environment and the people living in it.

3. Take your regular hygienic bath, substituting standard soap with the African black soap or coconut soap. Right after, take your spiritual defense bath and dry yourself.

4. Extinguish the candle without blowing it out, and break it into three pieces. You can either wave it in the air or use a piece of metal to extinguish it.

5. In a plastic bag or garbage bag, collect the broken candle pieces, the coarse salt, the charcoal, and the paper with your name.

6. Take the material collected in the bag immediately to the outside garbage. At that moment, all along the "bathroom-to-street" path, spritz the Green Spiritual Defense Spray, repeating the incantation:

"Envy and the evil eye,
You can't get me anymore!
Go away, disappear!
Go away and leave me here!"

The leftover spray can be saved and used as a perfume or air freshener. Spray it around your house, from the inside out, to break the negative energies surrounding it. Attention: This ritual must be performed at night, before going to sleep. You can reuse the pencil and plate normally.

Opening Paths

Unlock-All Bath

- Basil leaves
- Abre-caminho fern leaves
- Bay leaves
- Red pemba powder
- White pemba powder
- River or waterfall water
- Honey or molasses

Pemba powders are made from colored limestone chalk and are used in the rituals of Afro-Brazilian religions such as Candomblé.

In 2 liters of water, boil all the leaves, cover, and let cool slightly. In the warm mixture, add the pemba powders, river water, and honey. Wash your face, hands, and feet thoroughly, and then take a bath from the neck down. You can also use this recipe to wash the floor of your home or your work environment.

Open-Path Fumigation

- Dry leaves of rough-leaved pepper
- Dry abre-caminho fern leaves
- Dry rosemary leaves
- A handful of chicken corn (dried corn kernels)
- A handful of sunflower seeds

Sprinkle the well-mixed ingredients over red-hot coals and pass the smoke from outside into the house, asking for openness and victory in your paths.

Magic Soap for Progress

- 1 kola nut, dried and grated
- 1 grated bitter kola nut
- 1 grated aridan bean (fava de aridã)
- 1 grated nutmeg
- Powdered nut grass
- Powdered sandalwood leaves
- Powdered sage leaves
- Honey or molasses
- African black soap

In a mortar and pestle, mix all the ingredients to form a homogeneous paste, which should be kept in a clay dish or bowl and left in the open air for three nights of a full moon. After this period, take your usual bath using the mixture as a soap, three times a week, before the sun rises.

Prosperity

Roma Wealth Fumigation

- Powdered ginger
- 1 handful of sunflower seeds
- 1 handful of peas
- 1 handful of fennel
- 5 golden coins

Sprinkle the well-mixed ingredients over red-hot coals and pass the smoke from outside into the house, asking for financial growth, wealth, and prosperity in your paths. After it has cooled, blow the ashes and whatever is left of the fumigation into a busy town square.

Bring-Me-Money Powder

- 1 grated nut grass
- 1 grated nutmeg
- 1 teaspoon of powdered ginger
- 8 whole star anise
- 8 cinnamon sticks
- 8 whole cloves with the head
- 8 coffee beans or grains of paradise

In the oven, roast the star anise, cinnamon, cloves, and coffee beans; let them cool and pass everything through a grinder or crusher. Mix with the powdered ginger, nut grass, and nutmeg. You should prepare this powder on nights of a waxing or full moon and keep it stored in a glass jar or a red or gold velvet bag, and it must also be kept away from light as well as prying eyes.

Bath for Radiance and Recognition

- Artillery plant (brilhantina) or water hyacinth leaves
- 5 whole star anise
- 5 small handfuls of cloves
- 1 grated nutmeg
- 1 whole flower of wild sunflower
- African black soap
- Your favorite perfume (preferably from the bottle you are already using)

In 2 liters of water, boil all the leaves and seeds (including the whole sunflower), cover with a lid, and let cool slightly. In the warm mixture, add 3 liters of fresh water and five spritzes of your perfume. Strain everything and separate the flower. When bathing, use the flower as if it were a loofah, replacing your regular soap with African black soap. To rinse off the lather, use the already strained and warm bath—do not remove the lather with normal shower water!

Harmony and Bliss

Bath to Calm Children

- 5 white roses (only the petals)
- Cotton leaves
- Boldo leaves
- Orange blossom water or Florida water
- Honey

Mash the leaves and petals with your hands, mixing gently with the orange blossom water to let them macerate. Strain well and add the honey. This preparation can be used as a bath, from head to toe, or mixed into the drink of a very active and anxious child.

Bath for Insomnia

- Lavender leaves
- Boldo Leaves
- Colônia or spiral ginger leaves
- Rosemary leaves
- Lavender essence or perfume

Fill a clear glass jar with pure water and let it sit for at least 24 hours. Gently mash all the leaves with your hands and mix together with the water and lavender to macerate. Strain and take a bath in the evening, from head to toe. Let the leftover leaves dry in the sun and prepare a herbal pillow with them, which should be placed inside your regular pillow.

Fumigation to Bring Peace and Harmony

- Dry rose geranium leaves
- Dry peppermint leaves
- Dry lemon balm (Melissa) leaves
- Dry rosemary leaves

Sprinkle the well-mixed ingredients over red-hot coals and pass the smoke throughout your house, clockwise from the front door.

Love and Attraction

Catch-Husband Powder

- Dry coral vine leaves
- Dry Surinam cherry leaves
- Dry petals of a red rose
- Powdered patchouli
- 1 small piece of rolled tobacco (fumo-de-rolo)
- 7 whole grains of paradise
- A handful of pubic hair

Chew the grains of paradise, visualizing the person you desire, and without swallowing, mix the chewed grains with saliva and the other ingredients in a clay or earthenware bowl. Roast the mixture in the oven and sift until very fine. After it is ready, the powder should be mixed in the food or drink of your love, without their knowing. You must keep this ritual a secret—if you tell anyone you performed it, it automatically loses its effect.

Attractive Bath

- 7 red roses (only the petals)
- 1 handful of sunflower seeds
- Pure honey or crystal sugar

In 2 liters of water, boil the rose petals and the sunflower seeds, cover with a lid, and let cool slightly. In the warm mixture, add seven small spoons of honey or crystal sugar and take a bath from head to toe.

Passion Potion

- 21 basil leaves
- 21 roasted fenugreek leaves
- 9 drops of orange blossom water or Florida water
- 1 glass of river or waterfall water
- ½ glass of mild red wine
- 1 small shot of *cachaça* (sugarcane liquor) or rum

Hand-mash the leaves and extract their juice, and then mix with all the other ingredients to macerate. Store the mixture in a glass jar and leave it out in the open air of the full moon for three days, starting on a Monday. For three Fridays in a row, this mixture must be applied to the chest, after regular bathing, without drying it off.

Power Pots

Defense (Main Gate)

- 1 large black pot
- 1 medium piece of jute
- Expanded clay pebbles

- 1 chunk of sulfur
- 3 red pepper seedlings
- 3 gale-of-the-wind seedling
- 3 snake plant seedlings
- 3 iron spears

At the bottom of the pot, make a hole and place the jute and expanded clay pebbles, covering the outlet for excess water. Cover with soil up to half of the pot and place the chunk of sulfur right in the center. Fill with soil up to the necessary height to plant the seedlings: in the middle, the snake plant; around it, alternate the red pepper seedlings with the gale-of-the-wind seedling, planting one after the other, forming a circle. Position the spears diagonally, forming a triangle around the pot. When placing the pot at the gate, make sure that the triangle's base faces the house's front and one of the tips faces the street.

Break-Envy (Front Yard)

- 1 large clay pot
- 1 medium piece of jute
- Expanded clay pebbles
- 7 seedings of dumb cane
- 7 small mirrors, without borders

At the bottom of the pot, make a hole and place the jute and expanded clay pebbles, covering the outlet for excess water. Fill with soil up to the necessary height to plant the seedlings. Plant the dumb cane seedlings and top up with soil to the rim of the pot. Looking from the street toward the house, place the pot at the first point your eyes reach; in the pot's soil, forming a semicircle toward the entrance gate, position the mirrors so as to reflect the house's main entrance. Attention: If possible, assemble this directly on the ground of your front yard, eliminating the pot.

Leadership and Authority (Living Room)

- 1 medium pot made of red ceramic
- 1 plate or saucer to support the pot
- 1 medium piece of jute
- Expanded clay pebbles
- 1 railroad screw
- 21 citrine crystals (or enough to cover the pot once it is ready)
- 1 Dutchman's pipe seedling
- 1 sandalwood seedling
- 1 gale-of-the-wind seedling

At the bottom of the pot, make a hole and place the jute and expanded clay pebbles, covering the outlet for excess water. Fill with soil up to the necessary height to plant the seedlings. Plant the seedlings in the pot, symmetrically, forming a triangle, and fill the pot up with earth. Right in the middle of the pot, between the seedlings, bury the railroad screw until only the head is sticking out. Cover the surface of the soil with the citrine crystals without hiding the screw head.

Magic Kitchen

Golden Rice of Wealth

- 1 tablespoon olive oil
- 1 cup rice
- 2 cloves garlic, chopped

- 1 medium onion, finely chopped
- 1 teaspoon saffron or turmeric
- ½ cup raisins
- ½ cup chopped or sliced almonds
- Salt to taste

In a pan with hot olive oil, sauté the garlic and onion, add the rice, and let it brown. Add water to cook the rice and add the saffron or turmeric, stirring until well mixed. When it is almost dry, add the raisins and finish cooking. Garnish with the almonds and serve.

This recipe can be prepared at any time, preferably during a waxing or full moon. Regardless of the moon phase, it is one of the dishes that should *always* be on your New Year's table. Before serving, separate a portion while it is still warm and bury it in the yard next to the entrance gate.

Vegetable Milk for Seduction and Virility

- 1½ cup almonds
- 1 piece of fresh ginger
- 400 milliliters coconut milk
- 600 milliliters pure water

Carefully choose the grains or seeds, removing any possible dirt and debris; soak them in pure water for at least 4 hours or until softened, and strain. In a blender, mix the grains and water that were soaking, the coconut milk, and the ginger, beating until a homogeneous mixture is made. With a cloth filter or strainer, strain the mixture and put it in the refrigerator.

As with all magical love recipes, vegetable milk for seduction should be prepared during a waxing or full moon, but it can be consumed regardless of the moon phase. When using this recipe for a specific suitor, you both must share the drink. After straining the recipe, you can prepare a talisman with the leftover almond and ginger: place the dried mixture inside a red pillow, with the name of the two of you inside, and leave it under your bed.

Harmony and Friendship Cake

For the Dough

- 1½ cup sugar
- 1 tablespoon dehydrated lavender
- 1¼ cup unsalted butter
- 2 cups wheat flour
- 4 egg yolks
- 4 egg whites
- 1 tablespoon baking powder

For the Syrup

- ¾ cup water
- 1 tablespoon dehydrated lavender
- 2 tablespoons sugar

Dough Making

Using a mixer, beat the sugar, lavender, butter, and egg yolks until you get a light cream. Without beating, mix in the flour, the egg whites, and finally the baking powder. Pour the mixture into a greased cake pan and bake for 40 to 60 minutes in an oven preheated to 180 degrees Celsius (350 degrees Fahrenheit). Remove from the cake pan while still warm.

Syrup Making

Boil the water with the lavender for 2 minutes, like a tea. Turn off the heat, cover the pan, and set aside the mixture until it cools. Add the sugar to the already strained mixture and return to the pan to heat until a thin syrup is formed. Drizzle the cake with the hot syrup, let it cool, and serve in slices.

This recipe is excellent for relieving everyday stress and fatigue, and for balancing the emotional and spiritual energies of those who eat it, so avoid preparing it when the moon is waning. You can also prepare it to attract and strengthen friendships and create good relationships with people close to you; in this case, you can prepare it as a gift to a new neighbor or a friend you haven't seen for a long time, or to offer it at family or school reunions.

You can also substitute lavender with another herb or seed of your choice, observing the magical potential of each and adjusting the enchantments according to the desired goals. However, an important point is not to change too much the amount of herbs in the original recipe (neither too much nor too little), to prevent the dough from getting heavy after baking and making the cake not rise.

Magic Perfumes

The preparation of magic perfumes is quite simple and follows the same procedure for all recipes, as we learned in detail in the section "How to Create Your Magic Perfume" in chapter 18. From one formula to another, what changes are the chosen essential oils and the proportions of one oil to the other until, in total, you have 20 milliliters of the mixture of aromas (approximately 450 drops). The following recipes indicate the necessary quantities of each essential oil for the desired purposes. For the method of preparation, consult the previous chapters of the book.

Prosperity

- 55 drops of **clove** essential oil
- 55 drops of **cinnamon** essential oil
- 110 drops of **star anise** essential oil
- 110 drops of **sandalwood** essential oil
- 120 drops of **ginger** essential oil

Harmonization

- 55 drops of **honey** essential oil
- 55 drops of **lemongrass** essential oil
- 110 drops of **lemon balm** essential oil
- 110 drops of **lavender** essential oil
- 120 drops of **orange** essential oil

Relaxation and Meditation

- 55 drops of **lavender** essential oil
- 55 drops of **musk** essential oil
- 110 drops of **frankincense** essential oil
- 110 drops of **Surinam cherry (pitanga)** essential oil
- 120 drops of **lotus flower** essential oil

Spiritual Cleansing

- 55 drops of **rue** essential oil
- 55 drops of **eucalyptus** essential oil
- 110 drops of **rosemary** essential oil
- 110 drops of **lemon** essential oil
- 120 drops of **peppermint** essential oil

Love and Seduction

- 55 drops of **strawberry** essential oil
- 55 drops of **patchouli** essential oil
- 55 drops of **ylang-ylang** essential oil
- 110 drops of **almond** essential oil
- 175 drops of **red rose** essential oil

Roma Pots

Energy Filter (Drains and Toilets)

- 1 square glass pot 5 centimeters high
- Eucalyptus essential oil
- Cedarwood essential oil
- 1 kilogram coarse salt
- 1 concave mirror
- 7 amethyst stones
- 7 whole garlic cloves
- Rosemary, without the branches

Mix the coarse salt, rosemary, and 7 drops of eucalyptus oil, filling the pot almost to the top. Place the concave mirror over the mixture, right in the middle, and around it intersperse the amethysts and garlic cloves. Drip a drop of cedarwood oil over each amethyst. Place the pot over the bathroom drain or toilet tank.

This pot can be made on any day of the week, preferably during a waning moon. When the coarse salt begins to solidify, throw everything out away from home and redo the ritual, reusing the glass pot.

Prosperity (Main Room or Office)

- 1 cylindrical glass pot, 40 centimeters high
- 1 kilogram lightly roasted chicken corn
- 100 grams white popcorn, already popped
- 1 package of honey candies
- 7 golden coins of good value
- 1 large pyrite stone

From the bottom to the top of the glass pot, interlayer seven layers of roasted chicken corn, seven layers of white popcorn, and seven layers of honey candy, symmetrically. On top of the last layer of honey candy, in the middle, place the pyrite with the tip facing up, and around it, place the coins in a circle.

This pot should preferably be made on a Monday during a waxing or full moon and positioned at the most central point of a living room, on the desk in an office, on the main counter of a kitchen, or on the cash register of a shop. When you notice that the popcorn has withered or that the chicken corn is turning to dust, throw it out in a busy street and redo the ritual, reusing the glass pot. If the corn rots, urgent spiritual cleansing should be done in the house.

Love and Seduction (Couple Bedroom)

- 1 round glass pot, wider than tall
- 100 grams dry hibiscus
- 100 grams sunflower seeds
- 100 grams rice in the husk
- 7 cinnamon sticks

- 7 chicken eggs, brown and raw
- 10 grams cloves
- 1 large crystal of rose quartz or amber
- Essential oil of red rose or patchouli

From the bottom to the top, in layers, fill the pot with the dried hibiscus, the sunflower seeds, and the rice in the husk. In the middle of the pot, on the rice, place the crystal and, with the cinnamon sticks, form a circle around it, anointing each of them with the essential oil. Sprinkle the cloves over everything. If one of the couple's members is a woman, intersperse the chicken eggs with the cinnamon sticks, anointing them all. If not, exclude the eggs from the recipe.

This pot should be made during a waxing moon, preferably on a Wednesday or Saturday. Keep it in the room for 28 days and throw it out in running water or a flower garden.

A Secret Tip

I really like to use dried herbs in fumigations and aromatic pillows, but I live in a very humid region, close to ponds and waterfalls. So, except for the last months of the year, when the heat is almost unbearable and the sun shines all day, I always ended up being held hostage by the weather. When I used to put the basins with herbs out to dry naturally, cloudy days meant more time to dry them ... and worse, rainy days meant losing all the herbs, which would get soaking wet. This was until I discovered an infallible technique for dehydrating the leaves without losing their magical characteristics or their aromas—and without relying on the weather for it!

First, grind the chosen herbs as much as possible and place them in a metal or agate baking dish. Heat the oven to medium temperature, put the dish with the herbs inside, and—*here comes the secret*—instead of closing the oven door completely, which would cause the herbs to bake and roast, using a piece of wood or a dishcloth, keep a gap open to let air through. This way your leaves will dehydrate entirely, and you can use them as you like!

Conclusion: From Now On...

After a long journey learning the powers, magic, and secrets of the sacred leaves, we have reached the end, and I want to thank you for your care and dedication to this point! It was an honor and a joy to share this knowledge with you, and I hope our story does not end now.

With that, I want to invite you to follow me on this journey, and to take the next step together. To do so, I have prepared another surprise for you: along with the *Sacred Leaves* book, you will also get free access to *a full online course with twelve classes*. You can attend them whenever and wherever you are through a computer, tablet, or phone, to deepen your knowledge and learn more about how to identify, classify, and combine the sacred herbs and plants to prepare your own power recipes to treat and harmonize various energetic conflicts such as love, prosperity, and opening paths!

To attend the online course is very simple: go to the website www.diegodeoxossi.com.br/classroom and register using the promotional code DDO-SACRED-LEAVES to create your username and access password.

To Write to the Author

If you wish to contact the author or would like more information about this book, please write to the author in care of Llewellyn Worldwide Ltd. and we will forward your request. Both the author and the publisher appreciate hearing from you and learning of your enjoyment of this book and how it has helped you. Llewellyn Worldwide Ltd. cannot guarantee that every letter written to the author can be answered, but all will be forwarded. Please write to:

Diego de Oxossi
℅ Llewellyn Worldwide
2143 Wooddale Drive
Woodbury, MN 55125-2989

Please enclose a self-addressed stamped envelope for reply,
or $1.00 to cover costs. If outside the U.S.A., enclose
an international postal reply coupon.

Many of Llewellyn's authors have websites with additional information and resources. For more information, please visit our website at http://www.llewellyn.com.